THE FIRST STONE

Some Questions About Sex and Power

Helen Garner

THE FREE PRESS

New York London Toronto Sydney Singapore

THE FREE PRESS
A Division of Simon & Schuster Inc.
1230 Avenue of the Americas
New York, NY 10020

An earlier edition was published in 1995 in Picador by
Pan Macmillan Australia Pty Limited

THE FREE PRESS and colophon are trademarks
of Simon & Schuster Inc.

Manufactured in the United States of America

10 9 8 7 6 5 4 3 2 1

Library of Congress Cataloging-in-Publication Data

Garner, Helen
The first stone: some questions about sex and power / Helen Garner.
p.   cm.
Originally published: Sydney: Pan Macmillan, 1995.
1. Sexual harassment of women—Australia—Melbourne (Vic.)—Case
studies.   2. Man-woman relationships—Case studies.   3. Power
(Social sciences)—Case studies.   4. Feminism—Australia.
I. Title.
HQ1237.5.A8G37   1997
305.42'09945'1—dc21   96–51063
                                                                CIP

ISBN 0-684-83506-1

Author's Note

When I began to write this book, the only names I changed were those of the two young women, since Australian law forbids the identification of the complainants in cases of alleged sexual assault. Soon, however, more and more people I had interviewed asked not to be identified. Now everyone in the text bears an invented name.

'The struggle for women's rights is . . . not a matter of gender loyalty. It is a matter of ethical principle, and as such, it does not dictate automatic allegiance to the women's side in any given argument.'

Zoë Heller

'Let the one among you who has done no wrong cast the first stone.'

John 8:7

THE FIRST STONE

A round lunchtime on Thursday 9 April 1992, a man
called Dr Colin Shepherd went to the police station
in the inner Melbourne suburb of Carlton. In the
CIB office there, he had this conversation with two
detectives.

~

– Mr Colin (sic), do you agree that the time is now
approximately twelve-o-six?
– I do.
– State for me your full name, please.
– Colin Shepherd.
– What is your age and date of birth?
– Fifty-four. My date of birth is 9 May 1938. Born in
Melbourne.
– Are you an Australian citizen?
– I am an Australian citizen.
– Mr Shepherd what I intend to do is interview you in
relation to two indecent assaults that have been reported
to the police . . . I must . . . inform you of (your) rights.
. . . Do you understand these rights?
– Yes, I do.

– Do you wish to exercise any of these rights before the interview proceeds?

– No. I am quite happy, thank you . . .

– Sir, could you tell me your occupation at the moment?

– I am Master of Ormond College at the University of Melbourne.

– . . . The term Master – what does that entail?

– It is the principal executive officer of a residential college of the university.

– Right, Mr Shepherd. Certain people have attended at this office and made statements in relation to certain allegations against you, and that's what I intend to speak to you about today. Could you tell me how many students usually live at the college?

– Approximately 320. The number varies a little bit.

– It's made up of both sexes, is it?

– Yes. At the moment it is fifty-two per cent male and forty-eight per cent female but it is always around about fifty/fifty, depending on who leaves or drops out or who does not accept a place.

– Right. Can you tell me how long you have been in charge of the college?

– Since the first of August 1990. A relatively short time.

– Right, Mr Shepherd. Do you recall a function being held at the college on 16 October 1991?

– Yes, it was the Valedictory Dinner, the formal final dinner for the year which the Governor of Victoria attended. It was a very splendid occasion, at the end of which the Student Club organised a party, what they call a Smoko, which was held in the Junior Common Room and the quadrangle of the college after the formal dinner.

It's a party with music, dancing, drinking and that sort of thing.
– Would you be able to tell me at what time approximately the dinner commenced and finished?
– The dinner commenced at about six thirty-five and would have finished about nine-thirty approximately. I am a bit hazy on the finishing time because of coffee after dinner and all that sort of thing, but the Smoko would have started about nine-thirty. It could have been a little bit earlier, but around about then.
– The Smoko goes through until a particular night hour?
– Yes – the alcohol must be turned off at twelve and music by twelve-thirty. There are college rules for those sort of functions.
– Right, sir. Are you able to tell me if you consumed any alcohol during the actual Valedictory Dinner?
– Yes, I did.
– Right. Would you have an opinion as to your state of sobriety at that dinner?
– Yes. I was well in control of myself. I had had a number of drinks because it was a long night, wine during the meal, but I had control of myself. I wasn't driving, because I live on the premises. I was also in very high spirits because it was a very successful dinner, a very successful function, and so I was in high spirits that night.
   I had had a number of drinks, but certainly I was in control of myself.
– Did you consume any alcohol at the Smoko?
– Yes, a little. I had a couple of beers and then I had some drinks in my room but that was nominal rather than actual.

– By the end of the entire evening how would you summarise your state of sobriety at that stage?

– Happy but not drunk.

– Would you have any opinion of how many people were actually at this dinner?

– . . . It's hard to give you an exact number . . . but I would say . . . in the vicinity of 280 people.

– . . . Would it increase or decrease for the Smoko? . . .

– Some ex-students tend to come back for that, in fact a number did . . . but there would also be some students who might not go on to the Smoko. Approximately 250 people I would expect to have been at that Smoko.

– Mr Shepherd, do you know a person by the name of Elizabeth Rosen?

– Yes, I do.

– Could you tell me how you know Elizabeth?

– I know Elizabeth because she was a student in the college when I arrived in August 1990. In the normal course of events I had not got to know her, (but) we did come in contact over disciplinary measures in September of 1990 . . .

– Perhaps if you give a summary of what you mean by disciplinary measures.

– Two major things occurred. Firstly, she was an unusual student in that she didn't perform any of the functions expected. For instance, students are expected to do student service, which means they do two hours a fortnight of table-serving or kitchen work. Everybody does that. It is part of the agreement of coming into college. In that way we spread the load of work and cut down the costs. So the students agree to do that. If by chance you cannot do your service on one night or day you should get a friend to do it for you. In the event that you just forget, you are fined. Now, (Elizabeth) had to pay a record number of fines, something like $750, for just refusing to do student service . . . Quite a substantial fine.

The second thing that happened was that when the students were going down for the vacation – that means leaving the college – they have to vacate their rooms, because we use the rooms for conferences. The cleaners came to me and said they had refused to clean one particular room, it was in such a disgusting state, and this was Elizabeth Rosen's room on the first floor of the main building. I and a number of other people inspected that room. It was in an absolutely appalling state. It hadn't been cleaned for some time. There were cigarette butts, broken glass, cigarette ash, obviously spilt alcohol in the carpet, which was a relatively new carpet. There were drawings on the walls and furniture, some of them in White-Out. We had to get the contract cleaners in to clean it. The carpet had to be replaced, the walls cleaned and in some cases repainted. I told her that she would have to pay the costs of all these contract cleaners, the new carpet, etc., plus I banished her from that room, at the time, to a very poor room – a room that it was regarded as a punishment to be in. She asked if she could go back, and I eventually relented; but she was punished in those ways.

So we had two major incidents with her, which put me on a bad footing with her, so she left at the end of that year. Now I am not one who likes to carry grudges. I've always tried to be careful to build bridges again, and I've always been very friendly to her since, despite that unfortunate conflict with her over those matters.

– Well, sir, Elizabeth Rosen alleges that whilst returning from a ladies' toilet at the Smoko at approximately 11 p.m., she made contact with you outside your office. Do you have anything to say about that?

– That's true, that's true. I was walking back to my office to escape the noise of the Smoko. My office is in the corridor just off the quadrangle and she happened to be there. We chatted. I asked her in and she came into my room. We spoke for about ten minutes. I offered her a drink which she took. I don't think either of us particularly drank it but I poured her a drink anyhow. So yes, that's true.

– Elizabeth Rosen further alleges that the conversation you had with her included her sister's application for attendance at the college. Do you recall that conversation?

– Yes, I do. She asked about whether her sister would be admitted. I tended to try and deflect that question, because it is not something you discuss with people, about (other) people's chances, in detail – but I indicated that if her sister had achieved well academically and met the criteria I saw no reason why she couldn't be admitted.

– Do you have a memory of closing the door behind you when you went to the office?

– Yes. It was a noisy corridor, and the noise from the Smoko meant that any time I went in there and talked to people I tended to close the door simply for noise prevention, to have a sensible conversation.

– Right. Do you have a memory, during the conversation, of hopping up and locking the door?
– I have a memory of the conversation and I did not lock the door. I certainly closed the door, for noise level, but the door was not locked.
– Elizabeth Rosen has also alleged that at one stage you turned off the overhead light, which left some sort of desk lamp on. Do you have any memory of that?
– No. The lights were on and the curtains were open, of that office.
– Do you have a desk lamp on your desk?
– Yes. That was probably on too. But there are two big lights, and the desk light, and the curtains were open that night so people outside the main building could see freely into my office.
– Elizabeth Rosen goes on to allege that you edged your chair closer to hers and were making references to her appearance, such as how beautiful she was and how attractive and that sort of thing.
– I deny that entirely.
– I also put it to you that during the conversation you made some reference to a photo.
– I don't recall that at all. I know the photograph that you mean. It's been drawn to my attention . . .
– Is that in fact a photo of Elizabeth Rosen?
– Yes. It doesn't look like a typical photo of her, in my memory of her, but it is Elizabeth Rosen.
– Did you make any reference to that photo in the conversation?
– No, I did not.
– Elizabeth Rosen alleges that you said, 'I often have

indecent thoughts about you,' referring to the photo. Do you have any memory of that?

– I deny it totally.

– I put it to you that the conversation continued, during which you said something to the effect of 'I really do have indecent thoughts about you,' and that then you asked her would she mind if you made an indecent approach to her. Do you have any memory of that type of conversation?

– There was no conversation of that type whatsoever. I can recall the conversation we had, and that was not part of it.

– I put it to you that at one stage you got off your chair and got down on the floor and grasped Elizabeth Rosen's hand.

– No, I did not leave my chair except to leave and get up and walk from it.

– I put it to you that Elizabeth stood up from her chair and that you then stood up and moved your hands from her hands to her breasts.

– Absolutely not. I didn't make any contact with her body whatsoever.

– I further put it to you that Elizabeth indicated that she wished to leave the room and you said something to the effect of 'Can I have a real kiss before you go?'

– Absolute nonsense. I said nothing of that kind whatsoever.

– I put it to you that after the conversation Elizabeth left the room.

– Yes.

– You left at the same time.

– Yes. I returned to the party, I think.

– Did you have any other contact with Elizabeth Rosen
during the evening, at the Smoko?
– Yes. I think it was before the discussion in the room.
I recall talking to her a couple of other times. In the
quadrangle and in the Junior Common Room with other
people.
– I put it to you that during the course of the evening
you approached Elizabeth at least four times. What do
you say to that?
– I can't recall how many times I would have talked to
her, or what you call 'approaching' her, but I certainly
spoke to her a couple of times. As to the number, I
would not know. I spoke to many students that night,
some of them many times, some of them a few times.
I couldn't recall how many times.
– I further put it to you that on one of those occasions
you placed one of your hands on her – what she calls her
bottom.
– I deny that emphatically.
. . .
– Are you able to offer any idea why Elizabeth Rosen
would make these allegations against you if they are not
true?
– Yes. I don't think I will elaborate on them. As I have
said, we have had a history of disciplinary conduct
together. That and other factors, I think, account to me
why that would be the case.
– Are you aware of a person called Nicole Stewart?
– I am indeed. She is currently a student at the college,
living though in a house in Parkville.
– So she's actually not a resident in college?
– Technically she is, because that is a college house, but

she actually lives in one of our houses in Parkville, rather than . . . living in the buildings on College Crescent.

– . . . Is there some situation with Nicole that she is not actually a paying student? Is she subsidised by the college in some way?

– Yes. Yes . . . she receives . . . this is very confidential – I don't know whether – I can explain what it is but I don't want to breach her confidence, do you follow? . . .

– Do you recall seeing Nicole at the dinner?

– Yes, I do indeed.

– Do you recall seeing Nicole at the Smoko afterwards?

– Yes.

– I put it to you that on one occasion at the Smoko Nicole was dancing with a group of friends . . . I put it to you that you . . . joined a group of Nicole's friends while they were dancing.

– Not quite . . . The Vice-Master and I were both in the quadrangle, and were persuaded not to be spoilsports and dance. I am not a keen dancer or a good dancer, so it was with some reluctance that both of us were persuaded to join in and dance. Having done that, I have forgotten who I danced with. I danced with a number of students during that period. This was early in the Smoko. Nicole Stewart offered to dance with me. It was what I would call distance mode, in the first instance. In other words she was three yards away gyrating rather vigorously and I was standing back looking very foolish. So certainly she danced with me.

– Right.

– And I can complete the whole story there. The Vice-Master was next to me in this group. There were a number of couples dancing, then the music changed to more slow-style dancing, or different style, which required traditional dance hold. We danced for approximately a record, whatever it is, three or four minutes, and then I danced with somebody else.

– I will just read you a passage from Nicole's statement, and then put that situation to you. 'I could feel that there was pressure where his hand was being raised up my back. He then moved his right hand across my ribs and placed it flat against my left breast.' Do you have any memory of that action at all?

– I deny that emphatically. I did not do that. My hand was on her back, at that stage of traditional dancing. My right hand was on her back, my left hand was holding her right hand, and that was it.

– I further put it to you, from Nicole's statement, 'His right hand cupped my left breast. His hand was completely covering my left breast and he was applying pressure as he did this.'

– I absolutely deny that totally. I couldn't do that because my right hand was on her back.

– I put it to you that Nicole moved your hand away from her breast and placed it back at her waist. Do you have any memory of that?

– I totally deny that that took place. It was a normal traditional dance. She was certainly a very vigorous dancer and I am not a good dancer – but we just stood and shuffled around a bit, from my point of view.

– Right. I put it to you that after she placed your hand back on her waist area, the same thing happened again – reading from Nicole's statement: 'I placed his right hand to the rear of my waist. He did the same thing again. He again kneaded my back as he raised his right arm up my

back, and his right hand came across my ribs over to my front and he placed his right hand over my left breast, exactly the same as before.'
– I totally deny that.
– And that again you applied pressure to her breast.
– Absolutely not.
– Did Nicole break from the dance? Or did the dance simply finish?
– No, the dance simply finished. And then I danced with somebody else, and she danced with somebody else.
– Did you notice any change in character or . . . emotions from Nicole from the start of the dance to the finish?
– None whatsoever. Not only that, but I had no knowledge that night of any untoward action at all, or that she felt there was – and I didn't know about it till (the following) March. In the days that followed there was no complaint or indication whatsoever . . . (until) on the fourth of March, a document headed COLIN SHEPHERD SHOULD BE SACKED was placed under everybody's door at the college, placed over notice-boards and circulated widely in the college and in the university. I became aware of the allegations and the people who were making them on the tenth of March 1992, when I was handed them by a solicitor, who was conducting an inquiry . . . for the college council.
– Do you have any . . . opinion . . . as to why Nicole would make these type of allegations if they are not true?
– No. No idea at all.
. . .
– Mr Shepherd, at this stage we are going to continue the investigation into the alleged offences. At some later stage you may be charged with indecent assault, with unlawful

assault. I just have to warn you again that you are not obliged to say or do anything unless you wish to do so. Whatever you say or do may be recorded and given in evidence. Do you understand this?

– I understand this and I deny the allegations totally and emphatically.

. . .

– Mr Shepherd, I am now obliged to put some questions to you in relation to fingerprinting.

One morning in August 1992 I opened the *Age* at breakfast time and read that a man I had never heard of, the Master of Ormond College, was up before a magistrate on a charge of indecent assault: a student had accused him of having put his hand on her breast while they were dancing.

I still remember the jolt I got from the desolate little item: *Has the world come to this?* All morning at work I kept thinking about it. I got on the phone to women friends of my age, feminists pushing fifty. They had all noticed the item and been unsettled by it. 'He touched her breast and she went to the *cops*? My God – why didn't she get her mother or her friends to help her sort him out later, if she couldn't deal with it herself at the time?' And then someone said what no doubt we had all been thinking: 'Look – if every bastard who's ever laid a hand on *us* were dragged into court, the judicial system of the state would be clogged for years.'

At this we laughed, in scornful shrieks. There was even a kind of perverse vanity in it, as among veterans of any tedious ordeal. It never occurred to any of us that a man accused of such an act might be innocent. But all that day

I experienced repeated rushes of horror. I didn't stop to analyse these feelings. I just sat down and wrote the man a letter.

> Dear Dr Shepherd,
>
> I read in today's paper about your troubles and I'm writing to say how upset I am and how terribly sorry about what has happened to you. I don't know you, or the young woman; I've heard no rumours and I have no line to run. What I want to say is that it's heartbreaking, for a feminist of nearly fifty like me, to see our ideals of so many years distorted into this ghastly punitiveness. I expect I will never know what 'really happened', but I certainly know that if there was an incident, as alleged, this has been the most appallingly destructive, priggish and pitiless way of dealing with it. I want you to know that there are plenty of women out here who step back in dismay from the kind of treatment you have received, and who still hope that men and women, for all our foolishness and mistakes, can behave towards each other with kindness rather than being engaged in this kind of warfare . . .

I posted this letter and went about my business, thinking that this would be the extent of my involvement in the matter. Like any other scanner of the local news, I followed the case with sporadic attention and the occasional sharp twinge of alarm. I noted that the magistrate had found proven the charge that Dr Shepherd had indecently assaulted the girl he was dancing with, but that no conviction was recorded; Dr Shepherd planned to appeal. Then, late in August, the second set of allegations appeared in the papers. They made painful reading, in the blunt language of the *Age* court reporter.

> The woman, a 21-year-old law student, alleged that Dr Shepherd assaulted her in his locked office during a late-night student party . . . The woman, who cannot be identified, has alleged that Dr Shepherd had locked his study door and turned the overhead light off. She said he had told her she was really beautiful, and that he fantasised about her photograph and often had indecent thoughts about her. She said Dr Shepherd cupped her breasts in his hands and squeezed them. Dr Shepherd denies the allegations. The woman alleged Dr Shepherd had asked her whether he could make 'indecent advancements' towards her. Dr Shepherd said this phrase offended him in its grammar and immorality, and he never used language of that kind.
>
> Dr Shepherd said he had spoken to the woman in his study. She had started the conversation in a bizarre way by provocatively asking whether he would have her name, followed by the words 'for ever', tattooed on his body. Dr Shepherd said it was clear what reply she wanted, so he decided to call her bluff and say 'Of course'. He said he spoke to the woman about her course, and university and college matters, but it was an unsatisfactory and weird conversation because it jumped from one subject to another. 'I felt that she was very dazed and confused,' Dr Shepherd said. 'I was not exactly sure of the reason. I had my own theories.'

In denying the student's allegations that he had knelt by her chair when making these approaches to her,

Dr Shepherd produced evidence that because of a hip condition he was unable to kneel at all, 'even in church'.

Cross-examined by Dr Shepherd's QC, the woman said she had told Dr Shepherd that her three aims in life were to own a Ferrari, a diamond necklace, and for someone to have her name tattooed on them. She denied she had asked Dr Shepherd whether he would be so tattooed.

> She said her sister had applied to Ormond College and because she was concerned about harming her sister's chances she did not make a complaint about the incident to the college until early this year, after her sister was accepted. 'Going to the police was the last resort after the college had failed to deal with it adequately,' she said.

What sort of people could these be? On 2 September, the morning when the judgement was to be delivered, I got on a bus and went downtown to the Magistrates' Court.

The room was very small. People were shoving to get in. I couldn't see anything but the backs of strangers' heads. The magistrate took only a few minutes to announce his findings, in a muffled voice. He said that although he thought something had occurred to distress the young woman who had brought the complaint, doubt remained in his mind as to what had happened in the study. The student, he said, was a spirited, forthright person, with many friends who cared about her; and Dr Shepherd had led an unblemished life privately and professionally, and was highly regarded. The case came down to oath against oath; and Dr Shepherd received the benefit of the doubt. The magistrate dismissed the charge. The police were ordered to pay Dr Shepherd's costs of $15 800.

The footpath outside the court was thronged with camera crews and press photographers, cruising like sharks for meat. I was ashamed and walked away. As I stood on the corner of Russell and La Trobe Streets, a group of young women from the court drifted past me and waited at the lights. They were striking girls, stylish in the understated manner of middle-class university students; full-faced, red-lipped, long-haired, wearing flat heavy shoes. They moved on to the pedestrian crossing in loose formation, not speaking to each other. They looked vague and confused, as if they hadn't yet grasped what had just happened. I wondered if the girl in the study, and the dancing one, were among them. For the first time I felt sorry for the young students. They were of an age to have been my daughters. I wondered who was looking after them, or advising them. I asked myself what advice *I* would have given them. I thought, *They don't know what to do next.*

~

Anyone who is familiar with the inner suburbs of Carlton and Parkville knows Ormond College. It is the most spectacular (though not quite the oldest) of Melbourne University's residential colleges, a massive Scottish neo-Gothic pile across the road from the Melbourne General Cemetery. Crowned by a high, pointed tower, flanked by tennis courts and deep gardens and car parks, it is shielded from College Crescent by thick pittosporum hedges which blossom sweetly in spring. But Ormond is famous for more than its size and its beauty. It radiates power. Its foundations are deep in private patronage and in the Presbyterian (now Uniting) Church; it is the site of the Theological Hall, where clergy are trained; and it is a way-station, for the ambitious and privileged middle class, between the big Protestant private schools of Victoria and the professions of law, medicine, engineering and science. *Who's Who* is thickly studded with Ormond alumni. Ormond is an institution which cares about its reputation.

Non-university people are sometimes puzzled by the function of Ormond's resident tutors, of whom there

might be as many as fifty in any given year: like all residential colleges, Ormond offers tutorial classes additional
to the teaching provided by the university proper, but these
classes are not compulsory: they are an integral part of an
old dream – the college not as a glorified dormitory but as
a community of scholars.

Like many ordinary citizens I had often, over the years,
used Ormond's grounds as a thoroughfare on my way
to work or to the city, and around the time of Colin
Shepherd's trials I took up this habit again. I would ride
my bike along a lane fringed with old peppercorn trees,
behind a row of pale stone houses where the theology
professors lived, and through a wire gate on to the Ormond
grounds. The casual eye saw no signs of trauma. Hoses
swung their arcs over lawns and shrubbery, and in the
tall eucalypts magpies warbled. In the upper storeys of
the huge main building, windows stood open on a sunny
morning. Except for the odd overalled gardener, no one
was about. The students had bolted their breakfast and
rushed away to their classes at the university. This was a
place where people lived, and slept: a sort of home.

Once or twice, stirred by a vague curiosity, I chained
my bike to a post and pushed open the vast front doors.
The hallways, permanently chill whatever the weather,
were built on a scale so grandiose as to be almost comic,
like the haunts of robber barons. Photographs from earlier
eras had been blown up, mounted and hung along the
passage walls: black-and-white pictures of sombre sporting
teams, of the casts of Greek plays, of students puffing on
manly pipes beside open fires, or lounging insolently in
doorways with their hands plunged deep in the pockets of
high-waisted trousers which gave surprising prominence,

in several cases, to their genitals. The only women to be seen in this gallery of privilege (apart from a couple of intellectuals with Ormond connections, whose portraits had obviously been added as a recent afterthought under feminist pressure or by some committee with a guilty conscience) stood with clasped hands beside tables at which young men prepared to attack their food in the enormous, shadowy dining hall. These women wore white caps and large white aprons: they were maids.

Stepping in from the beautiful gardens, with their flowing lines and spring foliage, I felt the halls in their grandeur to be overwhelmingly masculine: spartan, comfortless, forbidding. I had to pinch myself to remember that Ormond College, though originally established for men and their needs, had been admitting women as resident students for *almost twenty years*. To the passing observer, the presence of women seemed to have left no mark.

On 21 September 1992, the *Age* reported that Colin Shepherd's appeal against the guilty finding on the dancing charge was to be heard that morning in the County Court. Again, I went, hoping to see the central characters in the drama, to learn something from their faces about what had brought them to loggerheads; and this time, though it was rather late in the piece to be feeling what Janet Malcolm calls 'the familiar stirrings of reportorial desire', some instinct made me put my notebook in my bag.

In the crowded hall outside the court I noticed a huddle of young women sitting on a bench. They were leaning forward, silent, intent on what was being said to them by a thin-faced, thin-bodied woman in her forties. I hurried past them, keen to get a seat.

The court was filling fast. The mood in the room was severe. Two sorts of people, caricaturally different from each other, stood out in the crowd: old, thin, grey-haired, grey-suited Ormond men with stern faces and upright spines, a type I had privately thought of, since childhood, as 'Presbyterian'; and young women (also some young men) with the fresh skin, free body language and easy clothes of students.

A middle-aged couple was seated close to the front. I could see only their backs, but from the attitudes and glances of the people around them, I knew they must be Colin Shepherd and his wife. The man's pale grey suit was stretched tightly across his bulky shoulders. His hair was whitish, thinning, fly-away. The woman had pinned up her long brown hair, but strands of it had come loose and rested against her neck and on her shoulders. On the man's other side sat a teenage boy. The angle of his neck and the shape of his shoulders in his suit resembled the man's: plainly he was the couple's son. The three of them sat motionless, speaking to no one, looking straight ahead, like people waiting for a church service to begin. They made a small island of stillness in the flurry of the court.

The first witness called was Nicole Stewart. She stepped gamely into the box, a slim, pretty woman in her early twenties, with dark eyebrows, and blond hair pulled back into a ponytail. She wore spectacles, pearl earrings, a red jacket. She looked physically slight, but her presence was impressive and firm: I had imagined an uptight ideologue, not this composed person. The only sign of agitation was that her hands looked purple, as if with cold. She stated that she was a fourth-year law student, and that at the time of the alleged incidents she had been studying arts/law at Melbourne University.

The barrister acting for Colin Shepherd was a dapper, fit-looking individual of forty-something. He drew from Nicole Stewart her account of the evening in question.

After the Valedictory Dinner, she said, she went to the Smoko in the Junior Common Room. She had not drunk any alcohol before the dinner, and the 'College red wine' served at the meal was not, she said, 'something I particularly enjoyed drinking'. Several people in the court laughed. At the Smoko, she went on, alcohol was being served from a bar set up in the quadrangle. There was music, but no food. She drank 'two small cups of cider', and spent this part of the evening 'talking, dancing and socialising'.

Then, at about a quarter to twelve, she saw Colin Shepherd in a corner of the Junior Common Room. Her friend invited Dr Shepherd to join their group of four or five people and dance with them.

Three fast numbers were played, then came a slow one. 'Dr Shepherd,' said Nicole Stewart, 'pulled me into a ballroom stance. He had one hand on the small of my back, and the other on my shoulder. Kneading as he went, he moved his right hand up my ribs, then placed it flat on my breast and squeezed it.

'I removed it, and placed it back down on my waist. But Dr Shepherd repeated the action. I was very upset at this. I said, "Excuse me – I have to go and get a drink." I went outside to my friends.'

At this point the judge interrupted to offer Nicole Stewart a glass of water. He asked her if she would prefer to be seated. She said, 'Could I have a seat, just in case?' The judge called for a spare seat, and Dr Shepherd's wife, in a strange reflex of helpfulness, looked around her as if for a chair.

'I found my friends,' Nicole continued. 'I told them that the Master had groped me, that he had grabbed my breast. I was worried that he would ask me to dance again, so I asked one of them to dance with him. I went back to the Junior Common Room.

'Ten minutes later, Dr Shepherd came into the Junior Common Room carrying two drinks. He appeared to be looking for me, to dance with me again. But my friend grabbed his hand and danced with him.

'I left the group, and talked for twenty minutes to other friends. I was very shocked. I was attempting to socialise with these people and not managing to.'

The QC asked her about Dr Shepherd's sobriety.

'He was inebriated,' she said, 'but not drunk. He was flushed, and unsteady on his feet.'

This struck me as a fine calibration of drunkenness, characteristic of someone who had been around drinkers: an Ormond student's estimation.

'I went to walk out to the quad,' continued Nicole. 'I sat on the front steps with my friend and talked about what had happened, about what I'd do. I wanted some time to myself. I walked home to my boyfriend, and told him what had happened.'

Now the QC really got to work on her. Into his tone, neutral so far, he introduced the acid that chills a listener's blood, casting doubt, as it is meant to do, upon the whole moral fabric of the witness. He pestered and nitpicked. He described with mock relish the food that had been served at the Valedictory Dinner. He addressed Nicole as 'Madam' with the sarcasm that can lie behind what men have traditionally called chivalry. And when he got to the nub of her allegations, he squarely challenged her.

'The first time,' he said, 'you didn't move away from him.'

'I didn't want to believe,' said Nicole, 'that someone in that position would have done that.'

The QC leaned forward and turned up his chin. 'Why,' he said, 'didn't you *slap* 'im?'

The word rang in the air, sharp as a palm against a cheek. My skin prickled; a ripple ran round the court. You bastard, I thought – every woman in the room could answer that question.

'I was financially dependent on this man,' said Nicole. 'Of course I didn't slap him.'

'You didn't walk away? Did you continue to dance with him?'

'He was holding me,' said Nicole. 'I wouldn't describe it as dancing. He was *holding* me. It happened very fast.'

'Why didn't you say, "Stop it! Don't do that!"?'

'I *thought*,' said Nicole, 'that by removing his hand I'd *indicated* that.'

The QC charged onwards. He plunged Nicole into a morass of confusing details about the whereabouts, in the Junior Common Room, of the dancing. Then he brought up the matter of Nicole's having asked her girlfriend for help.

'You said to your friend, "The Master's just groped me. Can you come and dance with him? I'm worried that he's going to try to dance with me again." He touched you twice on the breast – and you ask *her*, your "best friend", to dance with a man who's just groped you? A man, Madam, who was "inebriated"?'

'Inebriated,' insisted Nicole, 'but not drunk. She'd danced with him earlier, and he didn't give *her* a hard time.'

Now the QC attacked what he called discrepancies between her statement to the police and what she was saying to the court. 'You didn't say to the police, in February 1992, which hand of the Master touched which of your breasts. You didn't specify that you and the Master were dancing when the incident occurred.' He handed her the statement and she scanned it silently.

'He put his hand flat on my breast,' said Nicole, 'and cupped it.'

'*Cup?*' said the QC. 'You said *squeeze*.'

'You have to cup a breast,' said Nicole with a short laugh, 'in order to squeeze it.'

No one in the court shared her laughter. She asked for a break. The judge granted it. He was courteous to her, and watchful.

Next, the QC came in on another angle. It was explained to the court that since Nicky was a student whose place in the college was paid for by the Ormond Bursary Fund, the Master was the person she had to consult every year about the continuation and the amount of her bursary.

'You also,' said the QC, 'were employed part-time at Ormond College as a librarian, to help you.'

Nicole bristled. 'Not just "to help *me*",' she snapped. 'Others were employed too.'

'Just answer,' said the judge.

'You had a library job,' pursued the QC. 'In February 1992 you had a brief conversation with Dr Shepherd about your bursary. When you saw him around the college that summer, did you ever suggest to him that he'd done wrong at the Smoko? Did you say to him, "I don't feel comfortable conversing with you"?'

'No,' said Nicole. 'But I told the Vice-Master.'

'In the meantime, though, things had happened. Were you disgusted? Did you feel he should not have remained as Master? You had no respect for him any more?

But you asked him for a reference for your articles, in December 1991.'

'Yes, I did,' said Nicole, 'because I felt it would be strange if I didn't. But I didn't use it. I used the reference I got from the Vice-Master.'

The matter of Nicole's dress on the night in question was raised.

'You were wearing,' said the QC, consulting his notes, '"a black tight short skirt with a low-cut top".'

'With straps,' said Nicole.

'Otherwise no covering?' said the QC smoothly. 'And how was your hair, on that night?'

'It was out.'

'Not pulled back, in whatever you call the way you've got it today? I'm afraid I'm not very good at this type of thing.' He smiled at the court, a man bemused by the arcane rituals of women's self-presentation. No one gratified him by laughing.

The day after the Smoko, Nicole said, she told two senior women members of the college what had happened at the party. They advised her to do her exams first and then deal with it, and this is what she did. After her exams she worked over the summer in the library. She wrote a brief outline of the events, which a fellow-student took to the High Court judge who was then the chairman of the college council. Later she submitted this statement, plus a fuller one, to the 'Group of Three' sub-committee which had been set up by the council to assess the complaints. Wanting to go through all available internal procedures, Nicole had also seen the director of the Melbourne University counselling service. It was not till after the Group of Three submitted its findings to the council, upon which the council expressed full confidence in the Master, that Nicole had gone to the police.

A young woman who said she had been good friends with Nicole Stewart for three and a half years told the court she had seen the Master watching their group dancing at the Smoko, and that she had asked him to dance with them. The Master was reluctant, but accepted the offer, and danced with the group. The Master was still dancing when she went outside to get a drink. Soon Nicole Stewart came out and joined her.

'She asked me to make sure the Master was occupied – to keep him away from her. She said he had touched her, twice. I was shocked. She was very upset, flushed, repeating herself – bewildered and shocked. She tried to get people to come with her, to dance with the Master. I danced with him for as short a time as possible – less than a minute. Out in the quad, with other friends, we spoke about what had happened to Nicky. After half an hour, she couldn't stay at the Smoko. I talked with her on the front steps for half an hour, and then she went home. She didn't want to be walked home.' Asked about Nicole's sobriety, the friend replied, 'Approximately the same as mine – she was not drunk.'

Cross-examined by the QC, Nicole's girlfriend tried not to bite; but her tone developed, under pressure, into a kind of casual, slow insolence. She attempted sarcasm. The more she was prodded, the more bumptious she became, until one trembled for the girl, labouring to appear nonchalant.

The QC reminded her of two conversations she had had with Colin Shepherd over the summer that followed the Smoko. 'You made no allegations to the Master then, regarding Nicky?'

At this, the girlfriend blew her cool. She exploded.

'What am I gonna do – tell him *off*?' she cried. 'It wasn't *my* place to complain about these events! I found my conversations with the Master very embarrassing encounters. When we were in social situations, all I wanted to do was be polite and get away.'

A male fellow student stood in the witness box with his hands clasped and his eyes fixed on a distant point. His style was deadpan, his diction formal, his accent cultivated. He said he had seen Nicole Stewart dancing with Dr Shepherd, who had her 'backed up against a wall'. After this, he had seen Nicky talking to her girlfriend, 'angry, waving her arms, very red in the face'.

Some very eminent men spoke up as character witnesses for Dr Shepherd: a professor from Monash, the Vice-Chancellor of Melbourne University, and an Anglican bishop, purple-chested and wearing a big silver cross. Their testimony, though sincere, slid past in a welter of clichés. The women who spoke for Shepherd were less illustrious, but they made more of an impression because they were so upset. 'I look at men,' said a female colleague in Education at Monash for twenty-two years, 'with a more jaundiced eye than I do at women. I felt compelled to speak in defence of a man, this time.' She described Shepherd as 'courteous and gentle', a man who 'didn't stand over people or oppress them', and who had always 'looked after the less-loved students'. An earnest young woman, who worked as a secretary in a charity organisation and had engaged in glee club activities with Dr Shepherd, declared that they had 'practised alone together in a closed room, many times'; he was, she said, 'an utter gentleman'.

The judge, by now, was constantly shifting his wig around on his head, as if struggling against sleep.

Colin Shepherd at last took the stand. Like Nicole Stewart, he was quite different from my mental picture. He was heavyset, with a forward-angled neck and a slightly protruding top lip. He did not impress as powerful; if anything, he looked dogged, even meek. Perhaps he himself, when young, had been one of the 'less-loved students'.

Dr Shepherd told the court that before he took the Ormond post on 1 August 1990, he had worked full-time since 1969 in the Education faculty at Monash University. During this period he had been senior lecturer, Sub-Dean, and head of one department in the faculty. He had attended social functions involving the students he had taught, where alcohol had been available; there had been no accusations of impropriety before the current allegations.

The official guests at the Valedictory Dinner on 16 October, the night in question, had been a famous erstwhile Master of Ormond, by this time Governor of Victoria, and his wife. Dress, for this formal evening, was 'black tie, its equivalent for women, and doctoral robes for High Table'. A strict timetable had been worked out with the governor's aides, and was submitted to the court. The QC seemed to have an obsession with time-discrepancies in people's accounts of this immense, wandering, un-pin-downable saga of a party. 'The fruit cocktail,' said Dr Shepherd, 'was on the table, grace was said, the royal salute taken, then the fruit cocktail was consumed. A citrus fruit cocktail was picked because it doesn't go off.' Speeches were interspersed with courses throughout the evening. After the dining hall formalities, the official party was piped out of the hall, and assembled in the Senior Common Room.

'The governor and his wife,' said Dr Shepherd, 'left the function with my wife at ten-thirty. They went to their motor vehicle.'

After the departure of the official guests, Dr Shepherd and his wife went to his office and removed their academic dress. 'My wife retired, and I moved around the corridors talking to the students, specially the valedicts. There was a slide show in the quad, of the year's events. I met the Vice-Master in the corridor, and went to the quad with him, to the bar, where we had a drink. At the bar we were joined by other tutors and students.

'I was persuaded to join in the dancing. First I danced with a tutor, then a student kindly invited me to dance with her. While we were dancing I teased her – it was a light-hearted conversation – I pretended that I didn't recognise her without her glasses.'

Speaking levelly, without emotion, he went on to describe his dance with Nicole Stewart very much as he had done in his interview with the detective. The accusations of his 'kneading' and touching Nicky on the breast were, he said, 'totally incorrect'.

He spoke about his alcohol intake on the evening. He said he had started, but not finished, a glass of champagne and orange juice before the dinner. At High Table, where eight people had dined, one bottle of red wine and one of white had been served, he said, plus orange juice and mineral water. Dr Shepherd said that he himself had drunk two glasses of red wine and a lot of mineral water. He had drunk no port, though port had been served. After the governor had left the college, Dr Shepherd had drunk one beer 'in a plastic glass from the student bar'. After dancing he had drunk another beer, and further drinks in his office during the night. In his room he had had whisky but this had been 'nominal rather than actual'.

'My high spirits,' he said, 'had nothing to do with the drinks. They had to do with a very successful dinner.'

Several witnesses of modest demeanour declared their belief that Dr Shepherd had not been drunk at the Smoko. 'Effusive', yes, because the evening had gone so well – 'happy', but not drunk.

And then out of left field appeared another witness from Ormond College, a student with a ponytail. He was not at the dinner on the night in question because he was working at the Camberwell Kentucky Fried Chicken out- let. After work he took a tram back to Ormond, changed out of his uniform, and went down to the quadrangle. He had not entered the Junior Common Room at once, but had climbed on to a small bench outside it, and looked in through a window. He recognised the Master dancing with someone whose name he did not know. She was 'moder- ately tall, with blond hair of reasonable length, and she was wearing a black dress.' The length of this dress? 'Short.' The witness watched the Master and 'this female', as the QC put it, for several minutes. He couldn't say what kind of dancing they were doing, but thought it might have been 'both sorts'. He had had nothing to drink. He observed no signs of distress. He got down off his bench and left while the Master and the girl were still

34

dancing. This Mozartian figure with his queue, this passing Cherubino standing on a bench and peeping in at the
action, plays no further part in the story.

~

At 11 a.m. the next day, 22 September 1992, the judgement
was to be given. I arrived early and found a seat on the
aisle in the second row, right behind the broad back of
Colin Shepherd, who was once again accompanied by his
wife and son. A young student near me began to spread
her jacket on the chair beside her, to save it for a friend;
but two old men, whom I had seen the day before among
the phalanx of grim-faced Presbyterians, arrived at the end
of the row and saw what she was doing. One of them
called out to her in a stern, loud voice, 'You're not entitled
to do that!' Her smile faded. She quickly gathered up her
coat and moved along one place. The two old men pushed
past me into the row, shoving hard against my legs
although I tried to turn them aside to allow passage. Their
manner was so peremptory that I thought they must have
had a prior right to these particular seats, or needed to sit
behind the Shepherd family in an official capacity. I looked
up at the men as they forced their way past me, and said,
trying to co-operate, 'I'll get my bag out from under your
seat.' They did not answer, but stood in the row and
waited, blank-faced, staring into the distance, without the
slightest acknowledgement that a fifty-year-old woman was
down on her hands and knees among their legs, trying to
shift her belongings out of their way. Flustered, I sat down
again on the end seat. The men installed themselves at
their ease. One of them took out a newspaper, spread his
arms and began to read it, taking up so much space that I

was forced to lean sideways out into the aisle. They were completely unaware of my discomfort. These were 'Ormond men', then. They expected to be deferred to. I was in the way and they behaved as if I were not there. Much later I was informed that their aim had been to form a buffer between the embattled Shepherd family and people who had previously sat near them and muttered hostile remarks. As an unknown woman, I was told, I would have been '*prima facie* suspicious'. At the time, however, as I removed myself to a seat in one of the side rows, I noticed that my neck was prickling and my heart was beating fast.

The QC strolled into the courtroom. Seeing that the place was overflowing, he made a little *moue* of surprise, and shook his head, making his eyebrows into an inverted V, like an actor pleasantly surprised by the size of the house.

The judge took his seat and read the judgement, holding the paper up in front of his eyes as if he were short-sighted or wanted to hide his face.

Nobody, he said, saw the act in question. Nicole Stewart was 'an excellent witness' and he did not disbelieve her. She had an impeccable record for honesty. But he could not find Dr Shepherd guilty, because the allegations were not proved beyond reasonable doubt. It came down to a matter of oath against oath. The judge set aside the magistrate's decision, and found the appellant not guilty. He ordered that the Crown pay Dr Shepherd's costs for both hearings.

The court cleared fast. As the Shepherd family rose to leave, the son, a plump, pale boy of nineteen or so, having controlled himself as long as he could, suddenly burst into loud, racking sobs. The sound of his weeping echoed off the bare walls and the ceiling of the courtroom. His mother cried too, in the arms of one of the two grey-suited men. 'I can't believe she did it to him,' she kept saying over his shoulder through her tears; 'I can't believe she *did* it to him.'

Colin Shepherd himself looked stunned. The family's outburst of distress seemed to swallow up his feelings. His face was expressionless. What satisfaction could he find in such a decision? Did he believe he would get his job back, after this?

Outside on the cold street the students' solicitor, a dark-haired, solid woman who looked scarcely older than her clients, was telling journalists that two complaints had been registered with the State Equal Opportunity Commission. And then everybody walked away.

Now they were taking it to Equal Opportunity? But the EO approach to charges of sexual harassment is based on aims of confidentiality and conciliation: surely it was far too late for that. Shepherd might have been found not guilty by the court, but his name was being bandied about in the media, he had been stood down from his position at the college, and his professional reputation was the property of gossips. The story did not make sense. I felt the first stab of real, businesslike curiosity.

I went home and wrote Colin Shepherd another letter, asking him for an interview. His accusers I would have to approach more obliquely.

~

I had two female acquaintances at Ormond. One of them, Dr Ruth V—, who had invited me to her college apartment one afternoon years before and served me cake and

37

tea on pretty crockery, I had briefly glimpsed in the company of several young Ormond women outside the court, on the day of the appeal. But before I had a chance to call her, I ran into her husband in the lobby of a theatre. He said to me, with a look somewhere between challenging and hostile, 'This Ormond thing is much more complex than you probably realise.' Taking this as an invitation to inquire further, I wrote Dr V— a letter. I told her I had shot my mouth off early on, when all I knew was what I had read in the papers; I asked her if she would speak to me about the background of the story, for a newspaper article I wanted to write. She didn't answer the letter. I phoned her. She said she couldn't speak to me because of the EO hearing which was pending. I didn't know it then, but this was the last time Dr V— would ever speak to me.

Next I went to Ormond to visit my second acquaintance there, Michelle B—, a young tutor I had met when I sat next to her in the court; we had exchanged a few remarks. When I explained my purpose, she gave me the names of several other university feminists who had supported the complainants, and promised to pass on to Nicole Stewart and Elizabeth Rosen my request for an interview.

'Why are they so angry?' I asked her. 'Why did they go to the police?'

'These men in their fifties,' she said, 'are the last generation who haven't had to deal with feminists in their ordinary work. I'm thirty-six. In my student generation you wouldn't have rocked the boat. But these days girls don't put up with it.'

With what? What else was there in this story, beyond accusations of nerdish passes at a party? Did something really monstrous lurk behind it? If so, why hadn't it come out in court?

After my initial conversation with Michelle B—, she never answered any further communication from me: I wrote to her and phoned her in vain. Like Dr V—, she slid back into the faceless group of women in the wider university who supported the two complainants; I never saw her or heard her voice again.

That same month, in the spring of 1992, I took a job with *Time Australia*, reporting the trial of a man accused of having murdered his girlfriend's two-year-old son. The horrors I heard in the Supreme Court each day threw the Ormond story into merciless perspective. The luxuriant gardens, as I pedalled across them those mornings on my way to the court, became less and less real to me. They seemed the site of an absurd, hysterical tantrum, a privileged kids' paddy.

But the story haunted me. I began to notice that I was anxious about it. I wondered if something in me had shifted, without my having noticed. I had thought of myself as a feminist, and had tried to act like one, for most of my adult life. It shocked me that now, though my experience of the world would usually have disposed me otherwise, I felt so much sympathy for the man in this story and so little for the women. I had a horrible feeling that my feminism and my ethics were speeding towards a head-on smash. I tried to turn on this gut reaction what they call 'a searching and fearless moral inventory'.

Twenty years earlier, in 1972, I had been sacked from my teaching job for having discussed sexual matters with my young students at Fitzroy High School. I tried to work out whether my initial rush of sympathy for Colin Shepherd had been merely an upsurge of the rage I'd had to swallow at the time, when I'd been sent sprawling and had had to pick myself up and find another way of making a living.

I thought too that, at fifty, I might have forgotten what it was like to be a young woman out in the world, constantly the focus of men's sexual attention. Or maybe I was cranky that my friends and sisters and I had got ourselves through decades of being wolf-whistled, propositioned, pestered, insulted, touched, attacked and worse, without the big guns of sexual harassment legislation to back us up. I thought that I might be mad at these girls for not having *taken it like a woman* – for being wimps who ran to the law to whinge about a minor unpleasantness, instead of standing up and fighting back with their own weapons of youth and quick wits. I tried to remember the mysterious passivity that can incapacitate a woman at a moment of unexpected, unwanted sexual pressure. Worst of all, I wondered whether I had become like one of those emotionally scarred men who boast to their sons, '*I* got the strap at school, and it didn't do *me* any harm.'

The innocence or guilt of Colin Shepherd was to me the least interesting aspect of this story. What I really wanted to know was why the girls went to the police. You'd think this would be a simple enough question; but it turned out to be very complicated indeed.

Then, in October 1992, I received two letters from strangers. The first, written in an old-fashioned, forward-driving hand on sheets of lined foolscap, was from a Mr Andrew McA—, a member of the Ormond College Council. He told me he had been co-opted on to the Group of Three, the sub-committee set up in March 1992 to examine the students' allegations against the Master. Having seen a copy of my letter to Dr Shepherd and heard that I wanted to write about the case, he was eager to correct the 'factual inaccuracies' which had appeared in the press, and offered to speak to me at my convenience. The second came from a woman called Janet F—, the director of Melbourne University's counselling service. She said that a Monash friend had sent her a copy of the letter I had written to Dr Shepherd. 'I have a large stake in (this),' she wrote:

> I had been called in to attempt conciliation between the complainants and Dr Shepherd in February 1992, and subsequently I was subpoenaed to appear in his defence . . . The outcome for me has been devastating: the radical

feminists have pilloried me in *Farrago* (Melbourne University's student newspaper), and there have even been graffiti about me in the Baillieu (Library) loos. I have learnt about witch hunts. What happens to truth when rage and fear and ideological passions are on the rampage?

~

One spring evening, a few weeks later, I went across the grounds of Melbourne University to Parkville, a pocket-sized inner suburb where many academics and professionals live, to visit Janet F—. In addition to her work as a counsellor, she was responsible at the time for handling sexual harassment complaints that arose on campus. She is a tall, slim woman in her forties, with the unshockable alertness of the practised psychologist. She struck me as someone who had been around, perhaps suffered in her private life; who knew something of the world and spoke from that knowledge rather than from theory or dogma. Like many people who have become embroiled in this story, she has a deep sense of unease about it. She laid out her map of it with care.

She knew nothing about it, she told me, until six months after the Smoko, when the Vice-Chancellor offered her services as conciliator to the Ormond council, which was facing an awkward problem. She was unnerved by the anonymous leaflet that had been circulated throughout the college and the university, with its character assassination of Dr Shepherd and other Ormond men, and its wild predictions: '*If Shepherd is not promptly removed, he will commit offences of a similar nature or worse. If attacked by Shepherd, please – do not panic – call the police. There is no guarantee his next crime will not be rape or battery.*' It was clear at once to the counsellor that the case was already too polarised, and the allegations too old, for conciliation to be of much use; but she agreed to try.

When the High Court judge, then chair of the Ormond council, phoned her with the name of the senior college woman through whom she was to contact the two girls, Ms Vivienne S—, she 'sensed hostility between the judge and this woman. It was easy for me immediately to take her side, because I found him pompous. I felt he was uncomfortable about the whole business and wanted it to go away. I rang Vivienne S—. She was cautious, but we talked. She said she had tried to stand back from the students and let them speak for themselves.

'But when I saw the two women, I thought they felt as though they'd never had a chance to really say what their complaints *were* – as though they hadn't been *heard*. When they went to the Group of Three, they'd been formally warned that once they signed their complaints they were at risk of defamation. The group was doing what was proper, in warning them of this; but it would have seemed legalistic and intimidating. I think they felt that Shepherd, as a man, was part of the power clique, and that they were victims and vulnerable.

'Shepherd, when I saw him, denied everything. He felt as much of a victim as they did. He felt deserted by Ormond. He'd not been told anything about the nature of the complaints – the judge had only told him not to drink at student functions, and not to dance with the students. Next thing he knew, this anonymous leaflet was circulated – and at that point his world started to fall apart.'

Janet F— was impressed by the integrity of both Nicole Stewart and Dr Shepherd. 'Shepherd was very concerned about the women – that they mustn't be hurt. And I thought, you're a fool – you don't see how appalling this could become for *you*.'

'I saw the students a second time – and then on the morning of their third appointment, a woman rang and cancelled. One of the receptionists took the call. I tried ringing them. I left messages. But they didn't respond.

'The Group of Three by this time was frantic: they had a council meeting coming up, that they had to report to. I thought it was probably going to be fruitless, but I typed up a report. It explained what sexual harassment is, and how complaints are usually handled. I talked about how hard it is to really establish what truth is, specially when people are under pressure and the events happened a long time ago. People feel there's no way they can move from what they've said. Their memories get absolutely fixed, and you can't shift them. The truth's not *knowable*. I said I thought both parties deserved to be respected, but that I found it hard to understand why the women were so *angry* – much angrier than most people I'd dealt with in similar circumstances. I suggested they appoint someone to look into male-female relations within the college.

'And the next thing I discovered was that the women were furious with *me*. In their eyes I had suddenly turned into the same kind of ogre as Shepherd.'

A complex struggle ensued over Janet F—'s report to the college council, a benign document which breached no one's confidentiality and attempted only to calm the situation, which had clearly gone way beyond the reach of sane negotiation. The students' solicitor demanded the document under Freedom of Information and threatened to report Janet F— to the Psychologists' Board. The campus newspaper, *Farrago*, was edited that year by puritan feminists. Despite – or because of – its tone, it exerted a certain influence on campus; and when it cast aspersions on Janet F—'s motives for giving evidence at Dr Shepherd's trial, although she had obeyed the fundamental principle that 'as a counsellor you don't *ever* appear in court without a subpoena', Janet F— was distressed – not only at being smeared herself, but because of the damage the smears might do to her counselling service and to the students' faith in the university's sexual harassment procedures.

Janet F—, in short, had got sucked into the Ormond maelstrom. Two years later she was still extricating herself. A multi-national fashion magazine ran a piece on sexual harassment in universities which implied that she had lost her job over her handling of the Ormond complaints. Janet F— took out a defamation writ, and the magazine published a retraction and an apology.

Back in spring 1992, however, when Janet F— talked to me in her quiet house, she was as sad and confused as anybody about the ethics of the story. She knew that for the college council to declare the women's complaints had been made in good faith and at the same time to announce a vote of confidence in the Master was no solution. 'To the women the outcome was hopeless. Justice had not been served. To them it was not *fair* that the council should give such a finding and that after it Shepherd should still be there. I can see that point of view. But I can't accept that you then take him to court and charge him with sexual assault. To me that's so far over the top that it's appalling.'

'Why, then?' I said. '*Why* did they go to the police?'

She gave a big sigh. 'In some of the more radical areas of women's help services, there's a *maintain your rage* thing – a belief that the only way to overcome having been abused is to be angry, angry, angry. I think anger is a very important part of the healing process – but if you're stuck with the anger for ever, that's not healing. I keep wondering what was going on in Ormond that maintained their rage so much. Was it an ideological position, or were there other things the women were angry about, that made them want to pursue it?'

'Do you think this is a generation thing?' I asked. 'Is this rage disproportionate, or are we on the scrapheap?'

'Our generation was all about sexual liberation,' she said. 'But the women in their early thirties, who teach in universities now – they're angry at the notion that someone would *invade* another person, sexually. To them the whole thing is located in the discourse of power, and the abuse of power. They find it impossible to believe that a man would ever touch a woman's breast, for example, without knowing he was exerting power. And the new ideology is that sexual harassment is a crime. If you get the opportunity to punish someone, you really ought to.

'To me, sexual communication is so complex and difficult – harassment is always going to happen without people intending it to. But for the radical feminists, even for me to *hold* that view is counter-productive to the advancement of women. I'm "unable to perceive the oppression", or too simple-minded, or too sold out, or too old.

'I've been noticing, too,' she went on, 'over the last few years, that women who come to me for therapy feel it's a big deal to confess that they have fantasies involving dressing up in fishnet stockings or being into domination or bondage. They see these as non-feminist fantasies – they're *proscribed* fantasies. They see themselves as sick, for having them. But I say, if you can't play in your fantasies, where *are* you allowed to play? Isn't that one of the pleasant things about there *being* gender differences – that there are games you can play?'

We sat at the table and stared gloomily out into the dark garden.

I drove home late that evening thinking of the good fortune of my generation – no Aids, freed by the pill: we had a large, safe area, for 'play'. But feminists now, the ones who are making the most noise, seem to be consumed by rage and fear. Things are closing down, for them. The area where they can play has become so small that it's only a dot – they can hardly see it, let alone stand on it.

~

The morning after my conversation with Janet F—, the *Age* reported that Colin Shepherd had lost the support of the Ormond council.

> At a special meeting last week, a motion that the council continue to express its confidence in Dr Shepherd was lost. The motion was proposed by the chairman, who told the council that the vote, by secret ballot, was decisive. He is believed to have later told Dr Shepherd of the council's change of heart ... The council agreed that what transpired at the meeting would remain confidential.

Was someone on the council leaking to the press?

Several days later I called the students' solicitor and asked her whether Elizabeth Rosen and Nicole Stewart knew I would like to interview them. She said they did, but that it was not yet possible, in case the Ormond council made it a condition of the EO settlement that the girls not speak publicly about it.

She told me how pleased the girls were 'about the motion of no confidence – but maybe the council finally sat down and read the judge's statements and took them on board. The girls' aim was not to destroy Shepherd.'

So Dr Shepherd was only caught in the crossfire between the girls and the college? I found this hard to swallow.

I first visited Dr Shepherd on 24 November 1992, at the Ormond College Master's Lodge, a low, wide, cream-brick house with big windows, surrounded by a screen of garden, and backing on to College Crescent. Compared with the neo-Gothic main building of Ormond, it has an almost suburban feel, though its scale – slightly larger than human – gestures towards importance. Its colours are pale, it is full of garden light, its big reception room is pleasant to be in.

Dr Shepherd welcomed me at the front door, re-straining a keen golden labrador. When I addressed him formally he said, 'Call me Colin, *please*.' His wife, he explained, was at work as deputy principal of a small pri-vate girls' school in the eastern suburbs. Having been stood down from the Master's position while the charges went to court, he was spending his days in the house, trying to finish a history he was writing of the Lord Somers Camp. By 'in the house' he seemed to mean more than just sit-ting at his desk writing. He looked at ease domestically, and gave no impression of being embarrassed or reduced by his indoor status.

He sat me down at a large table and set himself up

opposite me behind a stack of bulging manila folders, with his hands clasped loosely in front of him, like somebody preparing to be interrogated. I was struck at once by his hands: large, square, suntanned, with well-articulated fingers: they looked like a pianist's hands. In court he had looked grey-faced, even brow-beaten; but face to face he was an agreeable-looking middle-aged man, carrying a fair bit of weight – a plump Anglican rather than a rangy 'Presbyterian'. His eyes were bright blue and his face was soft. His hair was grey-white, thinning and wispy on top. His voice was slightly husky, as if he had been talking a lot, or singing. I failed to see in him the marauding beast described in the anonymous leaflet. His manner was loose, informal, not controlled. Something about him was disarming, probably because he was so eager to disarm himself. He seemed to want to please – not just me (and my notebook), but everyone. I thought he was a man with a strong feminine side to his nature. (During our conversation I asked him which of his parents he had got on better with. His mother, he replied, without hesitating.)

He spoke at length, in great detail, and with feeling. I had expected bitterness, or at least irony; but his face, when he mentioned the ideas and plans he had for the college, lit up with enthusiasm, as if nothing had ever gone wrong – as if he would perhaps still be the one to carry them out. It was clearly a job that excited his imagination. He depicted himself as 'an evolutionary person' rather than an enforcer of drastic changes – but still someone determined to 'change the college culture', with its heavy student use of alcohol, and the repellent customs that still stream out of the big male private schools. Early in his time at Ormond he had had to get rid of certain 'yahoos – troublemakers with very bad records of drunkenness and abuse of women'. He and other college heads had succeeded in blocking an attempt by the famous Naughton's Hotel, where college students drink, to extend its bottle-shop licence to midnight. 'But it isn't sufficient just to outlaw things,' he said. 'You have to persuade people. I had long, painful negotiations with the Student Club about these things but their committee changes every year, so you're always re-inventing the wheel.'

Coming to the job straight from Monash University, with its tradition of vociferous challenges to authority and its powerful feminists, he had, he said, 'addressed feminist concerns' from the time he became Master. He appointed two female medical officers and a female librarian; and the two holders of the college's prestigious visiting Scott Fellowship during his Mastership were women – one of them a well-known Australian feminist novelist. Dr Shepherd had also, he told me, started to follow up aspects of college history, and to add photographs of women students to the displays in the corridors. Most ironic of all, in the light of later events, was his response when he discovered that Ormond had no policy on Equal Opportunity, and no 'grievance procedures'. To advise him on how to correct this, he had set up an EO committee, composed of tutors, students, and general staff, including cleaners, typists and maintenance people. Ms Rose H—, the resident tutor he had asked to head this group, was one of the college's senior women, 'an obvious person' for the job, and she accepted it. But it was not long before Dr Shepherd's relations with Rose H— struck snags. On one occasion he had been bewildered when she interpreted what he saw as a routine request, for her to provide him with background information about a visiting woman scholar in her field, as demeaning to her and to women.

A proposal was put to him for the creation of a senior woman's appointment, a Dean of women students; but Dr Shepherd did not at once comply. Firstly, he said, the budget at the time would not have stood the creation of another full-time appointment; secondly, though he favoured such a position eventually, he was opposed to the labelling of any position as just for women: 'It's too narrowing,' he told me. 'It's divisive. A woman takes a position because of her abilities, not just because she's a woman.'

A month after the Smoko, Dr Shepherd told me, he was summoned to the office of the High Court judge who was chair of the college council, and told that complaints had been made against him. The judge had not named the students who complained, but contented himself with a warning. 'He said, "You should be very careful. You shouldn't go to student functions. You should watch what you drink. You should *never* talk to students on your own in your office. However, the allegations have been withdrawn, so that's the end of it" – boomph!' Dr Shepherd went back to work shaken but unenlightened.

In December 1991, two months after the Valedictory Dinner and the Smoko, Rose H—, the senior woman with whom Dr Shepherd had had disagreements, suddenly resigned from her position as chair of the Equal Opportunity Committee. In her letter of resignation she referred mysteriously to certain 'events in college' which, she said, made it impossible for her to continue to serve on the committee. Dr Shepherd, puzzled by this reference, mentioned it in January 1992 to the Vice-Master, who said, 'I think it's the events after the Valedictory Dinner that's done this.' Dr Shepherd had not known what he was talking about.

In February 1992 the judge called Dr Shepherd again and told him that the allegations had been formalised, and that he had appointed a committee, the Group of Three, within the college to look into them. Next, in March, came the anonymous leaflets, 'literally thousands of them, circulated throughout the college and the university, on every notice-board, in every toilet.' The press picked up the story before Dr Shepherd was told what the allegations were and who was making them. It wasn't till 10 March 1992 that he found out the complainants' names.

'I was very surprised,' he said, 'because Nicole Stewart had been around the college all over Christmas, working in the library. I had seen her during that time and spoken to her, about her bursary and all sorts of things. She'd even asked me for a reference for her articles, just before Christmas, and I'd given her one. It was a great shock.

'I didn't speak to the press at all – but they were after me. "Real Life", "A Current Affair", Doug Aiton – you name it. Reporters came here, into the college grounds. Every time I moved out of the Lodge, I was followed by teams of them. My kids had a rough time. I was a prisoner in here.

'The next thing I got was a phone call from the police, asking me to come down and see them about complaints of indecent assault. My solicitor advised me to say nothing, but I said to him, "Look, I've got nothing to hide – I'm not frightened of talking."

'I told the police pretty well everything, in response to complaints from the two girls. But a lot of what I said was excluded, in the courts. It was ruled not to be relevant. I was horrified to realise how limiting the rules of evidence are. You can't raise certain things. The only thing that matters is: You're alleged to have made this indecent assault – did that or did that not happen? All the context is regarded as irrelevant. What I thought was my most compelling evidence couldn't be brought forward.'

'And what was that?' I asked.

'I think there was a conspiracy, very well orchestrated and organised. The actual allegations were the tip of an iceberg. When I say *conspiracy*, I don't mean people in coats under bushes – but an organised attempt by a number of people to get rid of me. On the night after I lost Nicole Stewart's case, some of the women who supported the girls had a big party in the college, to celebrate.'

There is nothing more certain to make a listener shift uncomfortably in her seat than theories of conspiracy. But before I could open the topic further, Dr Shepherd heard his two younger children come home from school. He jumped to his feet and shouted a greeting. They came into the room, two teenagers in private school uniforms, and he presented them to me with unabashed love and pride. He went out to the kitchen to make us some coffee, and the children engaged me in dutiful conversation, smiling. I asked the girl who played the upright piano that was in the room. 'Dad, mostly,' she said. When he returned with a tray of cups and some sweet biscuits in a cereal bowl, they wandered away to their rooms.

Having read the police interview and seen Dr Shepherd being examined in court, I was filled with a mixture of embarrassment and boredom at the prospect of asking him to repeat the Smoko story yet again.

'Can I ask you about the night in question? What are your memories of it?'

'My memories of it are very good,' he replied promptly. 'My memories are better than most people's.'

So they may have been, but I had to keep steering him back to that painful topic; he had a tendency to swerve away from it, particularly in response to my mention of certain college members who he feels have betrayed him. In my interview transcript there is a huge, eight-page swerve, here, between my question and his answer to it.

'Sorry,' he said at last. 'I'm terrible. Well – I danced.' He went on to give an account of the evening that differed from the officially recorded one only in the conversational tone he used with me. It sounded like the same party all right, in its general shape and duration, as the one I had heard Nicole Stewart describe in court; but the landmarks were different, the mood was milder, and the crucial events that the women alleged were simply absent from it. To keep a balance in my mind, as he spoke, between all the versions of the evening I had heard, each one with its convincing circumstantial details and apparent sincerity, was beyond me.

'After it all finished at one o'clock,' he said, 'I went to bed. Woke up at the normal time next morning, six o'clock, took the kids to school at seven-thirty. A normal day.'

He stopped talking, gave a little shrug, and looked at me

with no particular expression on his face. I didn't know what to say. What was I doing here, in this man's living room, asking him to account for himself? I wished I could change the subject, or ask him to play something on the piano. To conceal my discomfort I asked him what he thought of the media coverage of the story.

'The media's what tipped the scale for me here,' he said, 'to push me out. The reason people on the council voted against me is because of the publicity – that's what's made my position here untenable. The meeting where they made the vote of no confidence in me was so confidential that when my solicitor rang up to find out what the motion was, he wasn't allowed to be told. *I* wasn't told. And yet a council member rang the *Age* and told it to the same reporter who was covering it earlier.

'It's damaged my reputation forever. There's been a lot of talk about me being in situations of power over attractive female students. Look – I've been teaching in schools and universities for twenty-seven years. I had pass or fail power over students – power over their future as teachers. There's never been a single item of untoward behaviour. My record was impeccable. What power did I really have over Elizabeth or Nicole? Elizabeth was an ex-student. Nicole was on a bursary, yes – but it was covered by a formula. I couldn't have refused her funds for personal, arbitrary reasons. This alleged power I was supposed to have over these people is an illusion.

'In terms of career I'm finished. My concern now is just getting a job, enough to keep the family happy. My age is against me – I'm fifty-four. Times are bad for jobs.'

'Do you really think your name is terminally smeared?'

I asked. 'I mean – do you think people believe in their hearts –'

He cut across me. 'There's a senior post going in an Education faculty. What they want is almost written for me. I've applied. But I can tell you they won't have me, because of this. People keep pointing me out, in the street. Other people make jokes. The worst are the really bad male chauvinists, who go "Ha ha ha – I do that all the time, but *you* got caught".'

Apart from having seen Nicole Stewart give evidence in court, all I knew of the two young women in this story was from hearsay. So when my research turned up a couple of black-and-white photos of the students, I examined them as carefully as if they contained coded information that I had to decipher.

Nicky Stewart's head-and-shoulders shot is technically and emotionally almost neutral, as if taken for a passport or a driver's licence. It shows a young woman in a black V-necked top, with smooth, shoulder-length blond hair. Her head is tilted forward and slightly to her left, perhaps to allow the silky hair to clear the eye. She is smiling, looking straight into the camera, showing only a tiny glimpse of teeth. Her eyes, which look dark under the finely arched brows, snap with intelligence: the alertness in this pretty face belies her conservative pose.

Elizabeth Rosen's photo, the one she claimed Colin Shepherd talked about during their conversation in his office at the Smoko, is from a different planet. The first impression it creates is one of shining. Then one notices the amount of flesh that is being permitted to shine. The gaze, whether one is male or female, drops like a stone from top to bottom of this photo, then travels slowly up. She is wearing a dark, strapless evening dress, out of which the double mass of her splendid bosom – the only possible word for it – is bursting. Her face and shoulders are tanned, her eyes are glowing, her dark-lipped, enormous mouth is split wide in a frank grin, showing perfect teeth. Her face is so dazzling that her hair, worn up and back except for one free curl over her right eye, is only a shadow. It is impossible not to be moved by her daring beauty. She is a woman in the full glory of her youth, as joyful as a goddess, elated by her own careless authority and power.

The sight of this photo administers a jolt to men and women alike. First they laugh, in shock. Then the women sigh as they gaze, and the men make lewd remarks – the kind of lewdness that makes women impatient with them, since its function is to conceal from themselves their deeper response, which is something like awe.

~

Towards the end of November 1992 I wrote each of the young women a letter, asking if they would speak to me once the EO conciliation was over. I said it was not my aim to take sides or make judgements, though since we belonged to different generations our views would tend to differ. I said I wanted to unpick the story and make more complex sense of it than the press had so far been able to. I said that without their experiences, feelings and views I would not be able to write a piece at all. I added that I had a daughter their age, and that it was as much for my own peace of mind as anything else that I wanted to speak to them. I posted these letters to the most accurate addresses I could track down.

Writing this now, I am amazed that I didn't go straight to the addresses I had, and knock on the door. It would be nice to think that good manners or journalistic ethics restrained me; but the truth, I admit, has more to do with middle-aged women's fear of their daughters. They despise us for the scruples and the patience we have had to learn from life. They have stolen from us the crude nerve of youth, and in their unmodulated vision of the human things whose subtleties we have learnt to respect, they charge past us and rush out to fight, calling it politics. This is natural and right. But it is painful; and in the face of their scornful energy we become timid.

~

Early that summer I phoned the complainants' solicitor. She was very frosty with me at first, as she told me that no date had yet been set for the EO conciliation. I told her I had written to the young women.

'Yes,' she said sharply, 'they rang me as soon as they got the letters. You must realise, Helen, that this thing is not being played out for the benefit of *your* finer feelings.'

There was a tense pause.

'I gather,' I said, 'that you don't think I should have written to them.'

'The girls were a bit appalled that you had their names and addresses,' she said, heating up.

'Their names? But I was in court!'

'It's illegal,' she said, 'to publish the names of complainants in these cases.'

'Illegal?' I said crossly. 'What have *I* done that's illegal?'

'Don't get *defensive*, Helen,' she said.

I took a couple of breaths. 'I'm not. It's just that I don't understand what you're telling me.'

She became courteous again. 'I'm saying it's illegal to pass on the names of the complainants – to identify them. Of course the whole college community knows who they are; but for anyone to pass on their names and addresses to you is an illegal act. Also, someone on the council has been leaking its meetings to the press.'

'Who would *that* be?' I said.

'I don't know. It's the wrong thing to do. I wish I had a crystal ball, to know what the college will do. The girls have been incredibly well-behaved. Other people I was at university with, if there'd been this level of anger, would have been running around doing graffiti or hate mail. But we said to these women, "Do you want to work through the law, or go to the media?" They said "The law", and they've stuck to it. I respect them for that.'

The leaks to the press from someone on the council, then, which started way back in March 1992, even before the complainants went to the police, had been purely coincidental? I said nothing, nor did I mention the abusive leaflet which had been distributed throughout college and university on 4 March. Nobody supposedly knew who was responsible for that leaflet, yet after its distribution, there was no course but war.

~

I was chatting on the phone with a magazine editor I had been working for, a graduate like me of Melbourne University.

'The older generation of men,' she said, 'the old blokes in the philosophy department, for example, when we were

61

students – if they did the things they talked about doing, they'd be in jail.'

'What sorts of things?'

'Oh . . . just the presumption of what women are *for*. As I heard an old journalist say, "I don't know what all the fuss is about – it's one of the rights of office." *Droit de seigneur*.'

~

I tried to recall the experience of being *harassed* – as distinct from *assaulted* or frankly *attacked* – by a man, the actual quality of the experience. I remembered something that happened to me nearly thirty years ago, on a daytime train from Melbourne to Geelong. I was reading in an empty compartment. The door opened and a man came in. He smelt of beer but did not appear dangerous. We sat in the compartment as the train rolled across the grassy plain. I seem to recall that it was a sunny day. He struck up a conversation. He was in his forties, probably, not particularly bright or stupid, just a country bloke. I responded to his sociable overtures out of good manners – or rather, because I lacked the rudeness that is required in order to go on reading something that interests you while someone boring is trying to talk to you; and also out of the middle-class guilt inculcated in me by my male leftie friends at university, who were always saying to us girls, 'Don't be a snob. When workers whistle at you or say hullo, you should smile at them. You're no better than they are.'

The man in the train was rather drunk, but not at all frightening; he was just dull. He told me at great length about his experiences in horse training. He had two daughters my age, he said, who would be leading one of his horses in the Grand Parade at the Melbourne Show next spring. He asked me if I would like to lead a horse in the Grand Parade, a suggestion too laughable even to require an answer. All this time he was shifting closer to me along the seat. I try in vain, now, to remember the stages this incident passed through, between conversation and the moment when he put his arm round my shoulders and asked me to *give him a kiss*. I *let* him kiss me on the lips, out of embarrassment, or politeness, or passivity, or lack of a clear sense of what *I* wanted, which was for him to dematerialise at once. No violence, no threat of any kind was involved, no force: only a steady, almost imperceptible persistence. What stopped it was that somebody walked past the compartment and looked in. Suddenly I saw through that unknown witness's eyes what was happening to me, what I was failing to object to. I saw that it was absurd. And I slid out of his grip and left the compartment.

What was my state, that allowed me to accept his unattractive advances without protest? I was just *putting up with him*. I felt myself to be luckier, cleverer, younger than he was. I felt sorry for him. I went on putting up with him long past the point at which I should have told him to back off. *Should have?* Whose *should* is this? What I mean is *would have liked to. Wanted to but lacked the ... the ...* Lacked the what?

Women fantasise about what we will do if a bloke blah blah blah – but when one does, a strange passivity can swarm through us. Is this really happening? Or am I being over-sensitive, as women are so often accused of being? Surely he'll stop in a minute. Surely he can tell I'm only being polite, that I'm not liking it. How can he be so completely unaware that I'm actually hating it?

Why isn't he reading my mind?

Around the traps I ran into a journalist who had begun to cover the Ormond story for a Melbourne paper in August 1992 but had put it down when it went to EO and was delayed. Because she had researched it much earlier than I had, she had spoken to both Elizabeth Rosen and Nicky Stewart on the phone, before they had become guarded. The girls' solicitor, she said, had also been very frank with her, to the point of having accepted a phone call, while the journalist was in her office, and chatting and joking freely with the caller in her presence.

'She said to this caller, right in front of me, "Don't you think it's a bit inappropriate for *me* to be giving legal advice to someone on the council?" There was a lot of laughter. Then when she hung up she turned to me and said, "Just to show you what the mood is towards Shepherd – that was a member of the Ormond council – and he was saying, "Can we sack him? Can we sack him?"'

~

On Christmas Eve 1992 I called Dr Shepherd. He told me that the conciliation had started about two weeks ago.

'I don't know what was happening. I sat in one room

with my solicitor from eight-thirty till one-thirty. The Ormond business manager sat in another. The complainants with their barrister and solicitor sat in another. The complainants didn't speak to me. They weren't interested in me. They must know I'm going.

'Several weeks ago the Ormond solicitor sent me a letter telling me to resign in seven days. I replied that this was "grossly unfair", and they backtracked. Now I'm on leave, which gives me time to look for a job.' People at Monash, he said, who had been negotiating to get him his old job back, had withdrawn the offer after receiving some 'anonymous threatening phone calls'. 'I'm too hot,' he said bitterly. Another eminent university administrator was so upset by this that he 'arranged for a private business group' to hire Dr Shepherd. 'It's not really my kind of thing,' he said. 'Rather a right-wing sort of group. But whatever one might say about that administrator, he delivers. He does what he says he'll do.'

~

On Christmas Day I went overseas. I got back in March 1993. The complainants' solicitor eventually returned my many calls.

'I've been away,' I said, 'and I wanted to ask you what's happened in the story – where things stand now.'

A chill ran down the line.

'Well, Helen,' she said, 'I'm not at liberty to say. And that's essentially it.'

'Do you mean you're legally prevented from speaking to me, or you've just decided not to?'

'Legally.'

'What law is it, exactly, that prevents you?'

'Look – you'll just have to accept that that's the way it is.'

'Is there anyone who's not prevented?'

'No.'

'There's not?'

'Of course,' she said, 'you're perfectly entitled to ask anyone questions, but if they're acting correctly, *they* won't speak to you either.'

After a long pause, I said goodbye. This was the last time she ever spoke to me.

~

On 6 March 1993 *Truth* ran the headline: SEX CLAIM STUDENT 'DRIVEN TO DRINK'. The story related how one of the two Ormond students who had brought charges against Colin Shepherd had been up in the Magistrates' Court on five driving offences. She pleaded guilty to exceeding .05, disobeying a red light, exceeding 60 kph, not displaying P plates, and not carrying her licence. Her lawyer claimed that she had been 'immeasurably' affected by the experience of the court case, several months before the night on which the driving offences were committed. On the first three charges, the magistrate fined her a total of $400, with $42 costs, and cancelled her licence for twelve months. On the remaining two charges she was fined a total of $175 without conviction.

Later in March, someone sent the *Truth* cutting to Colin Shepherd in the mail, anonymously.

~

'Universities,' said a classics graduate in his thirties, 'have always been places built on neuroticism and timid aggression. But I'm surprised it's got this nasty at Ormond. Ormond's got that easy-come easy-go feeling – I didn't think anybody would *care* that much.' He told me that he had gone there to dinner one night, with his wife. 'She's got a sort of genial contempt for university colleges. Her father went to one, and wanted her to, but she wouldn't. During the meal she went outside; when she came back she told me a couple of young blokes had bailed her up out there and said, "You've got a nice set. You get an A." She was laughing. Just because that stuff's got the potential to offend doesn't mean it *does* offend.'

~

On 23 March 1993 the *Age* reported that an EO settlement had been reached the day before, between Ormond College and the two women students. The college had been obliged by the settlement to issue a statement in which it acknowledged that the women's complaints 'could have been handled differently . . . with more sensitivity and with a greater degree of apparent impartiality. The college,' continued the statement, 'accepts that the students acted honourably and brought the matter to the attention of appropriate persons in a discreet and mature manner. The college regrets any hurt and distress suffered by the students.'

The council also said that adequate policy and procedures, which would have allowed the complaints to be resolved within the college, had not existed. However, future complaints, it said, would be dealt with 'more appropriately'.

Dr Shepherd, according to the *Age*, had been asked by

the college solicitors to approve this statement before it was released, but had declined to do so.

> The two women, whose names cannot be published, said last night, 'We hope that the actions we have taken over the last eighteen months have ensured that women students who are sexually harassed will not be placed in the same vulnerable position in which we found ourselves'.

This remark struck me as dignified. I wanted to ask the young women about this vulnerability. Did they mean vulnerable to sexual harassment in the first place, or were they referring to their college's failure to give them a proper hearing? Vulnerable to what? Oh, I did want to ask them these questions.

~

At lunchtime that day I phoned, at the university where she worked, another of the Ormond women whose names Michelle B— had given me: Mrs Barbara W—. I identified myself and told her I was planning to write an article about the recent events at the college. There was a short silence.

'Now that the settlement's been reached and confidentiality's over,' I said, 'I wondered if I could have a conversation with you about the case.'

A longer silence. Then she said, in a tense voice, 'Helen – *no*.'

'Can you tell me why?'

She took a deep, quivering breath, and launched herself. 'I am *extremely* disappointed, Helen, that someone like you, someone in your position, should have taken the position you did on this matter. You have been incredibly *stupid*. You have been amazingly, *unbelievably* stupid. Coming out in public –'

'In public? I haven't made any public statements. How do you know what my "position" is?'

'*I've* seen the letters you wrote to Colin Shepherd!'

'How did you come to read those letters?'

'He photocopied them! *And* I read the letters you wrote to Nicole and Elizabeth. Can you *imagine* how your letters upset them? You must realise, Helen, that this story is *not* being played out for the benefit of *your* finer feelings. Do you realise how you *upset* the girls, by continually ringing them?'

'I've never rung either of them – I don't even have their phone numbers!'

'Well – you must have been ringing their solicitor, then,' she said in a deeper, more challenging voice. '*Have* you?'

She was working me as a headmistress works a fourth-former. I was having to take deep breaths, to control a wild desire to giggle – and hadn't somebody else mentioned my 'finer feelings'?

'Of course I've rung their solicitor,' I said. 'Why shouldn't I? What makes you so sure I've got a frozen position on this? What makes you think it can't be changed by argument? This is why I need to talk to you – because you know more about it than anyone else.'

'*Listen*,' said Barbara W— between clenched teeth. 'I haven't spent eighteen months of my life on a matter like this in order to talk about it with someone like *you*.'

Too amazed to speak, I let out a nervous titter.

'It doesn't matter *how* long you talk to me on the phone,' she said in a low, shaking voice. 'It doesn't matter whether your position is "frozen" or not. I'm *not* going to talk to you. Maybe in five years, when I've recovered – *then* I might consider talking about it – but right now, Helen, the answer is *no*.'

There was a breathless pause. I exerted massive self-control.

'All right,' I said. 'Thank you for giving me even this amount of your time.'

'That's all right,' she said stiffly.

'Well – goodbye.'

Silence. I hung up.

~

So this was how they got the Ormond blokes on the run. I was winded by the exchange. Nobody had taken that tone to me since I was a teenager. Her scathing reference to my 'finer feelings' echoed almost word for word the crack made by the complainants' solicitor. This path to Elizabeth Rosen and Nicole Stewart was plainly not only blocked but mined and ambushed. How could I write about these people if they wouldn't speak to me? This was the moment to put the whole thing down and walk away. But if I dropped it now I would never understand it – and for some obscure reason I needed to. The ruder and more secretive these women got, the more determined to retreat into their faceless group, the more curious I became. What sort of feminists were these, what sort of intellectuals, who expected automatic allegiance from women to a cause they were not prepared even to argue?

Like most people I functioned from day to day on a set of assumptions that I was rarely forced to examine: the adjustments I made under pressure of events were semi-conscious and usually motivated by a desire to avoid taxing mental activity. I was still skating along on ice that had frozen in the early seventies. But now I felt I was on the verge of finding out things that would cause an upheaval in my whole belief-structure, particularly where men and women were concerned, and the way power shifts between them. I was working so slowly that by the time I got anything coherent written, the newspapers would have got bored with the topic and moved on. I needed a purpose for the questions I wanted to ask. I would have to write a book. I had no idea how to do it, how long it would take, or whether what I eventually wrote would be publishable: I thought I would just keep ploughing forward, asking questions, taking notes, and see where I ended up.

That same afternoon in March 1993 I pedalled down to Queen Street, where the High Court of Australia has its Melbourne office, to interview the judge who had taken the chair of the Ormond council not long before the girls' complaints had come to light, and who had resigned from the position soon after. The judge, a thin man in tie and shirtsleeves, ushered me into his office, which had such a splendid view to north, east and west that I had to turn my back on it in order to concentrate. On what little wall-space remained between the bookcases and the huge windows hung several black-and-white photos of wigged justices.

I had to work hard, while we spoke, to counterbalance an extra sympathy for the judge into which Barbara W—'s barrage on the phone had thrown me. I kept reminding myself that if I had been a law student in her twenties, a Nicole or an Elizabeth bringing unwelcome complaints, his manner towards me might well have been less charming: that my knees would have been knocking. As it was, however, he was the soul of courtesy. He outlined at once three reasons for having left the Ormond council when he did: the limited time he had to deal with the extra work the council chairmanship involved; the political overtones of the matter of the allegations, which sat ill with his High Court position; and the potential conflict between the activities of investigative bodies and the High Court, which might be called upon to review those same activities.

Out of the blue, towards the end of 1991, a young woman had phoned him in Melbourne and asked to see him in order to discuss sexual harassment. Applying a lawyer's caution, he got his associate in, so as to have three people present. The young woman, Fiona P—, who was an Ormond student and not one of the complainants, was acting simply as an emissary. She produced several anonymous statements, which contained certain allegations.

The judge told Fiona P— he would like to see the women who had made the complaints: it is written on every lawyer's brain not to act on hearsay allegations, let alone ones that are unsigned. Off she went, to arrange for them to come. Some hours later, on the same day, she rang the judge and told him that the students had changed their minds – that they wanted him to *tear up the statements*. The judge refused to do this. He asked her to return, bringing the women. Later still the same day, the judge received a phone call from the college Vice-Master, saying that Fiona P— didn't want to return, because the judge had been aggressive.

The judge called Dr Shepherd and told him that allegations against him had been made. He said that, though he himself would not proceed on the basis of anonymous allegations, and though he would not disclose to Dr Shepherd the precise nature of the allegations, he thought Dr Shepherd should know that they existed. Some months later, the judge was informed by another council member that there were now two complainants, and that they were not going to go away. Nicole Stewart had already signed her complaint, and Elizabeth Rosen, who had not been among the initial complainants, had now emerged with her statement, and entered the story.

Within forty-eight hours of getting the second round of statements, the judge stressed, he had formed a group of three council members to deal with them, and had made a point of including in this group one woman who, he was sure, would be far from uncritical of the college. The only way to get to the complainants by this time was through one of their supporters, Vivienne S—. The complainants would not come to a meeting of the Group of Three at the downtown law office of one of them because they said it would be 'intimidating'. Here the judge gave a laugh of genuine bafflement, perhaps, I thought, at the idea that a law office might 'intimidate' these young women and their supporters who, so far, had given the impression of being anything but shrinking violets. To get around this problem, the meeting was held in a borrowed, neutral room in the city. Present at this meeting were the complainants, the members of the Group of Three, and Vivienne S—.

Soon after this, a Melbourne colleague of the judge had faxed to him the abusive leaflet which had been distributed throughout the university and the college, warning people against Dr Shepherd and accusing the council and the judge of delay in dealing with the complaints. The judge was incredulous and outraged. After the appearance of this leaflet, the women's supporters had placed a statement on the college notice-board dissociating their informal investigating group from the production of the

75

leaflet. The judge had found this odd, since there had been no suggestion that the women's supporters had been implicated in it.

Around this time, the Vice-Chancellor of Melbourne University had offered to the Ormond council the conciliation services of the university's counselling director, Janet F—.

The judge was puzzled by the vigour with which the complainants had pursued the case. He admitted that before these incidents he had had little awareness of sexual harassment in general, though his wife, he said, had experience of it. Even the term 'procedures', in this context, had been foreign to him until recently. He remarked with a perplexed distaste that in the United States there seemed to be a doctrine that the family is inimical to the feminist cause, and that motherhood exploits women. He had also seen, while swimming in the Beaurepaire pool at Melbourne University, posters on display which encouraged women to ask themselves whether they had been sexually harassed.

During our conversation he returned several times to Fiona P—'s request on the phone, after her meeting with him, that he *tear up* the statements. He made it clear to me that he felt very strongly indeed that it was not proper to make complaints of such a serious nature, ones that could wreck a man's life, and then to withdraw them five minutes later with no explanation.

As I pedalled home through the remains of the summer afternoon, I thought that the High Court judge was certainly an honourable man, in the dictionary sense of the term: a man with 'a fine sense of and allegiance to what is due or right'; but he seemed to me also a man whom nothing had yet forced to grasp how deeply things have shifted between men and women in the modern world – or how women's notion of 'what is due or right' might be profoundly different from - and *inimical to* – men's. I wondered whether he had daughters. I longed to hear the students' version of their encounter with him – a version complete with tones of voice, body language, atmospheric shifts, all those details and quivers of meaning that men are notoriously so hopeless at delivering. It struck me too that the judge, like other men of status who have spoken to me about this story, had arrived rather quickly at the conclusion that one person lay behind all the trouble; and that this person was most likely to be a woman.

~

Months later, Fiona P—, the emissary who had taken the first complaints to the judge, spoke to me (by phone – she would not go so far as to meet me) across the *cordon sanitaire* that the complainants and their supporters had thrown up between themselves and me. Fiona, who had wrestled with her conscience for a long time before deciding to speak to me, struck me as a young woman of almost heartrending earnestness and decency. She had a blunt, breathless way of talking, and tied herself in knots throughout our two conversations, so determined was she not to name names or betray even the shadow of a confidence.

'The judge,' she said, 'dealt with me with *total* integrity. He spoke from good motives, though he was stern. I'm not saying he did a good job – but I didn't feel threatened by him. We didn't want him to *act* on the complaints – we went to him only to get advice – but he couldn't understand why the girls didn't want to sign them. They'd been advised that they shouldn't – that once they were signed they would become legal statements.

'I was a mediator. I volunteered. I'd never even had a conversation with the girls. I was a year younger than they were. I wasn't emotionally attached to them. Our thought was, "Can we work this out within the framework of the college?" – because a court's so *final*.

'It was so traumatic. It was sad that there was no *structure* – no one to go to, to tell us what to do. The student Equal Opportunity board at Ormond was a good idea but it was only at its starting-point. The EO group for all the colleges round the Crescent was basically males – and I wanted to keep it within Ormond. I didn't want to discuss it with Trinity.'

I put to her my question, which with every asking seemed cruder and less applicable: why did they go to the police?

'You make it sound,' she said rather desperately, 'as if it was all organised – as if we all knew what we were doing. But we didn't. I wasn't there any more – I'd gone overseas – when they decided to go to the courts. My involvement ended with the judge. What I really hated was the way everyone was boxed and labelled. Fellow-students were saying, She's *that* sort of girl; Colin Shepherd's *that* sort of man; he's *that* sort of judge. I got upset with the rumours about the girls, and when the media kept showing the harrowed figure of the Master. What *I* saw was everyone doing things with the best possible intentions. My role was to keep it out of the courts. I put a lot of effort into it. And I failed. I don't know if it was my fault – but I failed.'

~

On 25 March 1993 I wrote letters to all the women's supporters whose names I knew, and told them I had decided to write a book 'about recent events at Ormond College'. I said that I had been 'taken aback by the vehemence' of what Barbara W— had said to me on the phone, but that I accepted with disappointment that she, at least, did not want to speak to me. The only purpose of my letter, I said, was to inform them of my intention.

On 27 March I called Dr Shepherd and told him I was planning to write a book. After a brief pause, he pointed out that I was likely to have trouble with the defamation laws, but then added that he was quite happy with the idea, and hoped that the truth would come out; he said he had no fear of this. He said he had also, in mentioning the libel laws, not wanted to discourage me. He was now, he said, 'too hot to handle', and had no job and no prospect of getting one. I told him I had spoken to one of the women's supporters.

'Did you get an earful?' he asked.

'I did.'

He made a sound like a laugh, and said without venom, 'I believe they're at the root of all my problems.'

Whenever I've spoken to Colin Shepherd I've been struck by the absence of anger in his demeanour or tone. He shows rather a kind of stunned fatigue, and sadness; and sometimes bitterness.

I know a woman whose husband, like more than one man of otherwise reliable taste, harbours a nostalgic connection to Ormond. She is always shifting to the back of a dark cupboard the keepsakes he indulges in – prints, etchings, sentimental memorabilia got up by the college and sold to faithful alumni. The Ormond men she has met through his profession she finds 'opinionated, arrogant and ambitious. Only thirty years ago,' she said, 'when these blokes were students, they had *maids*. To clean up their *rooms*. Now they've got intelligent wives who mouth a few feminist platitudes but basically spend their lives looking after their husbands – lovely, soft, intelligent but basically biddable supporters.

'Once I went to an Ormond dinner with my husband. On my way to the toilet I stopped outside the dining hall to look at a big framed display of photos of the college support staff – the kitchen people, cleaners, caretakers, office staff and so on. I was thinking how good it was that these photos were on display, as well as the academic staff and those born-to-rule sporting heroes. And then a couple of old boys – fifty, fifty-five – also stopped and looked at the pictures. They started making jokes about them and sending up "this egalitarian business – it's absurd – getting quite out of hand". So I said, "*I* think it's *good*. It's a recognition that Ormond wouldn't be able to run without these people." They didn't even acknowledge that I'd spoken to them. They just turned and walked away.'

She went on to speak with a fascinated distaste about the building itself. 'It's got those sort of gatehouses with – what are they called? – *turrets*. And the fascistic scale of it! It's weird. I went to a wedding there once – they go back there, you know, to get married – and standing in that deep courtyard, the quadrangle or whatever they call it, I felt we were all completely cut off from the real world. It gave me the creeps. I thought, a place like this must *act* on people. Imagine the blokes it was built for, back in the 1880s – striding along the halls in their gowns and mortarboards – passing the port – desperately trying to convince themselves they weren't cast away – lost at the very bottom of the world.'

~

I mentioned to a businesswoman friend that I was finding out things I couldn't write without further damaging people who had already been hurt, on both sides of the fence.

'*Everyone* in this story must have been damaged,' she said. 'It's an overlay of one ideology on another. The very word *harassed* is maddening, to me. Women are all *harassed*. It goes without saying, like being *irritable* or *tired*. The thing is that men trivialise sexual harassment and women inflate it. Men make light of it and women make heavy.'

~

Early in April 1993 I received one reply to the letters I had written to the women's supporters. It was from a Ms Margaret L—, on the letterhead of the university where she taught. She identified herself at the top by means of her qualifications and position, addressed me by my full name, and went on to sort me out in firm and very formal language.

She told me she regarded my letter, in which I had told her I was going to write a book, as an attempt to intimidate her, and an instance of futile harassment. Her intention, she said, was to protect the women students from any further distress or harassment. She rejected with particular firmness any implication that she should reveal to me the confidences with which she had been entrusted. She wanted me to be very aware that *she had known*, for some time, of my efforts to collect information about this matter. As a parting shot she proposed to me as source material for my project the work of someone called Lance Peters.

I read this intemperate letter many times. I noticed that she used the word *harassed* about my having addressed her at all. So the world, to Margaret L—, was divided into harassers and harassed. If one were not completely with her, one was the enemy. It was not possible that someone who disagreed with her might have legitimate motives – or even be ready to be argued round. There was to be no discussion, no putting of a case. Also, she and her group owned the story. Who would tell it? Certainly not me – or not if they could help it.

One of my sisters suggested in her peaceable way that the letter's tone 'softened somewhat, towards the end – she gives you a useful research tip'. I had no idea who

Lance Peters was – some sort of theoretician, perhaps? – but I was sure that the linking of his name with mine was not intended as a compliment. I rang a friend at Melbourne University and asked her who he was. She said she had never heard of him. When I explained the context we both became feeble with laughter. She said she would go to the Baillieu Library and look him up in the catalogue.

It took me over a week to answer the letter. I put my reply through draft after draft. It mortified me that I was so exercised by the thing. 'It's not worth addressing yourself to *her*,' said a French friend, after an hour of close textual criticism under an oak tree in the Botanic Gardens. 'Address yourself to something *beyond* her. To the women who are experienced enough to have gone beyond fanaticism and hatred.'

On 11 April I posted my answer.

Thank you for your letter. I was surprised and sad that you saw intimidation, provocation and harassment in my three brief and (I thought) courteous approaches to you. It was as part of an attempt to put together a quiet, thoughtful account of the story and its wider meanings that I asked you for your version of the course of events at Ormond College over the past eighteen months. I know that it has been a difficult and painful time for everyone concerned, and I most particularly want to assure you that, contrary to your apparent impression, I never intended to urge you to divulge matters which have been entrusted to you in confidence. I respect the depth of your commitment to the complainants, and consider it unthinkable to expect you to betray their trust. Since this misunderstanding of my motive seems to have been fundamental to your refusal, I think that, having made myself clear to you on this point, I should now ask you again to agree to an interview, at a time convenient to you. I am asking this not only because your contribution to any account of the events would be invaluable, but also because I believe that we are both bound by our professions to encourage open discourse. It is crucial for both of us to maintain attitudes which permit the freest possible discussion of important things which happen in our community. This is why I sincerely hope that you will reconsider your decision. With best wishes . . .

A bit pompous, but I was getting bored. To be frank, scrub as I might, I could not quite scour out of myself a thrill of refined aggression, and a twinge of guilt for continuing to 'pester' her. Why should she, or any of these women, speak to me? But then I recalled that throughout the events somebody – at least one person – had been talking freely and in detail to the *Age* journalist, leaking the Ormond council proceedings to him, as part of a campaign. Yes, a cat may look at a king. So I sealed up the envelope more cheerfully.

∼

A young woman graduate of Melbourne University now working for an international publishing company told me she thought the 'extremity' of the Ormond complainants' response must have been an expression of their powerlessness – a rage at not being listened to. 'Even to make people listen to them they had to work themselves up and say, "But it was really, *really* upsetting!"'

'It's to do with the age at which you come into your power,' she said. 'And it's something to do with being Australian. We don't even seem to like being *looked* at. We take it badly. But women in other cultures *like* it. I used to argue for hours with a Frenchman, once, when I was just out of university and still very ideological, about the outrage of being looked at – the male gaze, and so on. But now I'm aware that I can say no. Or yes! – which is exciting – rather than going "Oh *God*! He's *looking* at me!"'

There are looks and looks. I remembered a lonely 'New Australian', as we called them in the fifties before they transformed our society, who sat on the edge of the timber promenade at the Eastern Beach swimming pool in Geelong, one summer afternoon, and watched me with a burning concentration while I played alone on a float that was bobbing in the calm water. His attention broke into my happy play (I must have been about fourteen) and made me self-conscious and ashamed. (There it is again – the word *ashamed*. What is it doing here?) He did not speak to me, or make gestures, or try to draw my attention to him. He just watched me. I was not prepared for this. But is anyone ever prepared for it? Was it his fault, my parents' fault, my teachers' fault, society's fault? Is 'fault' a helpful way of thinking about his gaze and my discomfort?

Or is language, rather than looks, where the problem lies? A friend described to me a scene she once witnessed in a café down at Bondi. Near her sat a gorgeous young woman dressed in light, revealing clothes, having a coffee with a girlfriend. She had a fine body and beautiful breasts and she sat there in her beauty, proud of it, ready to be looked at by the world. At a nearby table sat a bunch of bikies. They stared at the young woman, couldn't take their eyes off her. The atmosphere in the café, at first, was light, zingy, appreciative: a mood of wordless, flirtatious play. But then one of the men called out something to the beautiful girl. My friend didn't hear what he said, but she felt the atmosphere turn sour. The girl swung round and shouted back to him, 'No – they're *not* silicone.' The mood was broken. The room was full of aggression and offence – but, my friend stressed, only after words had been used. 'It's as if,' she said, 'there were no *language* for appreciation.'

I placed a flurry of phone calls.

The Vice-Master of Ormond was down at the river-bank at the women's inter-collegiate rowing, 'a very important event', as the female secretary lightly remarked.

Mr Andrew McA—, the member of the Group of Three who had volunteered to speak to me, remarked irritably, when I rang him, 'The council seems set on a course of action which is completely unjust.' His impression was that practically everyone at the party had been drinking on the night in question, and 'wouldn't have known whether they were Arthur or Martha'. He had seen the report in *Truth* about the drink-driving conviction of one of the complainants, and expressed outrage that her name should be protected while Shepherd's was made public again.

The Women's Officer of the Melbourne University Student Union, Christine G—, agreed to speak to me about the Ormond story. I described to her the kind of 'quiet, thoughtful' book I wanted to write. 'Yes,' she said, 'this does seem to have burst out into areas that were ... unwarranted.' She was apprehensive, though, about saying things that the complainants wouldn't be happy about, and said she would try to contact them before she spoke to me. 'Would you like me to do that?' she suggested warmly.

My heart sank. Like all requests, this one would no doubt have to be processed at the faceless supporters' Checkpoint Charlie. 'That wasn't my aim in approaching you,' I said hastily, 'but if you think it's a good idea . . .'

~

One of my sisters said to me, 'Now that the lava has spread out across the countryside and begun to cool, some of the people involved in the explosion must be looking back and thinking, "My *God*. How could I have acted the way I did? How could I have got swept up in all that madness?"'

~

While I was sorting through the mass of papers I had so far collected, I came across a photocopy of Elizabeth Rosen's statement to the EO Commission. She might not yet speak to me, but here was her voice, though mediated by some representative of something or other:

'As a result of Dr Shepherd's actions, Ms Rosen felt like "a worthless sexual object"; and was "humiliated and powerless to control what was happening to her".'

I sat and looked at this for a while. *A worthless sexual object.* The phrase *sexual object* I was, of course, after twenty years of involvement with feminist rhetoric, familiar with to the point of being blind to its peculiar psychology. But *worthless* sexual object? The phrase gave me the little shiver one gets when confronted with the disingenuous.

Why would a young woman feel 'worthless' when a man makes an unwelcome sexual approach to her? She might not *like* it. She might want very much for it to stop. But why does it make her feel 'worthless'? Would she feel 'worthless' if the man were younger, better-looking, more cool? Or is *worthless sexual object* just a rhetorical flourish, a bit of feminist sabre-rattling on behalf of a young woman who has not taken the responsibility of learning to handle the effects, on men, of her beauty and her erotic style of self-presentation?

Can a young woman really expect to go through life without ever having to take this responsibility? Has a girl like Elizabeth Rosen even the faintest idea what a powerful anima figure she is to the men she encounters in her life? She told the court that Dr Shepherd had got down on his knees before her. Which of them does the word *humiliated* apply to, here?

~

'Sexual harassment's always going to happen,' said a young university graduate, 'but it has to be more acceptable for women to get *angry*. There needs to be some protection against being made to feel uncomfortable. I take uncomfortable feelings due to sexual harassment *seriously*.

'Once, when I was about twelve, I was asleep on an overnight train to Sydney. I woke up and found a man stroking my face. It was the bloke sitting next to me. I got out of my seat and ran away. I spent the rest of the night standing up, near the toilets, where people go to smoke. Next morning he came out and apologised. He was about thirty, I suppose, looking back. I was' – she made a shrinking gesture with her whole body, rounding her shoulders inwards, dropping her face right down as if to hide it – 'I was *ashamed*, I think.'

'Why should *you* have been ashamed?' I said.

We looked at each other in silence. I can't count the number of times the discussions I had with women reached this point, and got jammed.

Uncomfortable, though – this lily-livered, half-arsed word looms very large in sexual harassment discourse. *Uncomfortable* is made to do duty for proper, accurate words about feelings. A child who wakes up on a train and finds a strange man stroking her cheek is not *uncomfortable*. She is shocked, panicky, defenceless.

~

The only woman member of the Group of Three told me on the phone that she could not speak to me. 'I'm bound by confidentiality,' she said, in a slightly trembling voice, 'because I'm still on the council. It's still red raw as subject matter, at this proximity. It's roused enormous passion and bitterness. Perhaps if the court results had been clearer . . . There are people on both sides with barrows to push.'

P eter M—, the Vice-Master of Ormond, is a pleasantly spoken, smiling man of fifty or so, who on the day I visited him was dressed in grey trousers, a striped shirt and tie, and the good-quality brown brogues with a sheen that are favoured by men in this college milieu. He has the sprightly manner of the very experienced private school master he was before he came up from a provincial city to take the Ormond job; and how often must he have looked back with longing to the genial racket of the classroom, once he became aware that he was occupying one of the hottest seats in this drama.

Having been named as one of four sexual harassment officers for all the residential colleges, he was approached on the morning after the Smoko by Fiona P—, a member of the Student Club General Committee – later to become the emissary to the High Court judge – who reported to him 'a sexual harassment incident involving the Master'. She told him nothing specific, not even the name of the student who had made the complaint. All she wanted from him was advice on how to proceed.

'I was prepared,' he told me, 'to speak to Colin Shepherd on the spot. I told the student I'd be prepared to do so *that afternoon* – that if she wanted me to do this she should let me know.'

Fiona P— returned later that morning with news of another incident from the Smoko, and asked him not to speak to the Master yet. 'Often the perpetrator of sexual harassment,' said the Vice-Master, 'is unaware that harassment has taken place. We were hoping that conciliation would let everyone concerned come out of it with dignity. I think the complainants wanted to *hold* it' – he made a passionate cradling gesture against his chest – 'to *contain* it, at that point.

'So I didn't speak to Colin.'

~

Now this is one of the hinges of the story. Dr Shepherd must have been sitting virtually on the other side of the wall while Peter M—, the Vice-Master, discussed the complaints with Fiona P—. What if he had gone straight in there and laid the whole thing on Shepherd's desk, before dinner on the day after the Smoko? Could it have been sorted out to everybody's satisfaction within twenty-four hours? If the students had been cool enough to repeat their statements to Colin Shepherd's face, to ask for an acknowledgement and an apology, might Shepherd, even if he felt utterly certain that he had not done the things they accused him of, have found in himself the *sang-froid* to *do the gentlemanly thing*? – to say, 'I certainly don't remember doing what you say I did, and I can't believe I ever would have done such a thing – but we'd all had a bit to drink – I was over the moon because the dinner had gone so well – if I seem to you to have behaved inappropriately, I'm terribly sorry – I hope that you'll accept my sincere apology – and that none of us will ever need to speak of it again'?

This is the pragmatist's fantasy of a way out. It rests on a presumption of worldliness in all the protagonists. It assumes fundamental generosity, flexibility, good will, an absence of fear, a willingness to *go the extra mile*. It assumes that though the things the students alleged might well have happened (this being an imperfect world), and might have given offence, they were not, ultimately, earth-shattering; that a man might not necessarily feel himself backed into a tight corner by such allegations, since foolish things done at parties are not after all so rare: if they were all to be punished, which of us should 'scape whipping?

But it fails to take into account a certain kind of modern feminism: priggish, disingenuous, unforgiving. And it ignores one important fact: that in order to seize the nettle, the Vice-Master would have had to betray the trust of Fiona P—, almost before she was out of earshot. His position, at this juncture, must have been ethically excruciating. But some of the older Ormond men have spoken irritably to me about Peter M—'s silence at this stage. One of them, whose own behaviour in the matter conspicuously lacked grace, used a term of such high-handed condemnation that I thought I had misheard him, and said, 'Pardon?' He looked me right in the eye and repeated the phrase, enunciating with such force that he showed his teeth. This was one of many moments, in conversation with Ormond men, when my blood ran cold.

~

Soon after this crucial decision not to take the complaints straight to Dr Shepherd, Peter M— was disturbed to find that two other members of staff already knew about the complaints, including one senior woman who 'had seen herself as often having to be an advocate for women's position in Ormond'. Before long, said Peter M—, he was 'side-lined'. He had been twisting in his chair as he spoke. Now he began to draw deep sighs.

When Fiona P— came back upset from her 'legalistic situation' with the judge and the unsigned complaints, Peter M— felt for her anxiety. 'She was getting dragged in over her head. There's a limit to what a fellow-student can do – and she wasn't anxious to return in the afternoon, with or without the complainants. So I rang and told the judge she would not be reappearing that afternoon. He indicated to me that he would speak to Colin. A fortnight later, the day after the Carol Service' (this is how Ormond people measure time) 'I rang the judge to check – well' – he grimaced, and corrected himself – 'to *inquire* whether he'd seen Colin. He said he had.

'In December the senior woman chair of the EO committee Colin had set up resigned. When she told him why, he had no idea what she was referring to. When I realised this, in January, I thought, this has gone far enough. I went into his office and explained that the complaints were of sexual harassment on the night of the Valedictory Dinner.

'He was *rocked* by this. From this I gathered that the judge had spoken to him only in generalisations.

'In March 1992, round about the time of the Commencement Dinner, a hurtful leaflet was distributed. The judge wrote a statement about the whole matter and it was pinned on to the Hall door. Only half of it was read out.'

He had dropped suddenly into the passive voice. I asked,

taking a punt, 'Why did you read out only half of the statement?'

'I'd discussed it,' he said, 'with one other council member. I read out the most relevant bits – what the judge had done about the unsigned complaints. I read it out in the vestibule. Two hundred people were milling about in there, wanting to get into the dining room to eat. I didn't want to go on and on – but I certainly didn't attempt to conceal anything.

'This thing had an effect on the people working here. It's very difficult for secretaries, the office staff, who want normality in their working routines. They were undercut by a feeling of disturbance. They were certainly not helped by the coming and going of barristers and solicitors to Colin Shepherd's office. There was a sense of something going on. It would have helped if the legal advisers had gone to Colin's house.

'Colin was anxious, but he's always presented – not a brave but an optimistic front. He hasn't wavered. But neither side has moved at all. It's a great tragedy. It's hard that Colin was named and the complainants weren't. The damage is already done, though he's been cleared by the courts. I try to' – he wiggled his flat hand – 'sit on the fence. Because I have to deal with both sides. It's all right for the tutors. They've got the university as well, they've got other priorities. But if you're here all the time you see the devastation. To a man and his family.'

~

I went straight from the Vice-Master's office on to the Melbourne University campus, to speak to Christine G—, the outgoing Women's Officer of the Student Union. She was a chic young woman in black, very composed, with clear pale skin, a severely pretty haircut, and a bright dash of Poppy lipstick. I took a breath to remark in a friendly tone that in my young days as a feminist we would have died rather than wear lipstick; but I held my tongue, sensing (correctly, as it turned out) that she would not appreciate a joke – not on that topic, anyway, and certainly not from me. The warmth of her manner on the phone had congealed into the permafrost of a feminist who'd been shown my letter to Colin Shepherd. She pointed to an armchair with its back to the door, and took her place in front of her computer terminal. In order to look at me she had to turn her whole body sideways, which gave me the awkward feeling that I was interrupting her in some more pressing task. Still, I asked her my forlorn but crucial question: how and why did the police get involved in this case? She answered me with a firm statement.

'The procedures here didn't lead to justice. All the different avenues were tried – but there were structures which protected Colin Shepherd and the college itself.

'I'm not regretful at all. There are too many absolutes in the Melbourne University sexual harassment procedures. For example, women have to go through conciliation. There are too many conflicts of interest. The director of counselling, as an employee of the university, is *necessarily* compromised. She can be approached as a counsellor *or* as a sexual harassment officer – but she can't be both.'

I asked her why conciliation was such a problem for her. She shifted in her seat; the mood in the room stiffened and became wary.

'The procedures at the moment,' she said, 'are structured so that you get an apology and you get the behaviour to stop – and that's all.'

'Isn't that already quite a lot?'

She looked at me narrowly. 'I'm against people having to go through conciliation before there can be retribution.'

'Retribution?' The Old Testament word took my breath away.

'If you want some form of justice,' she went on, 'for the harasser to be *punished*, you're seen as asking too much. You're being "nasty".'

'What sort of punishment would you envisage?'

'In the industrial award for academics,' she said, 'there's a clause that deals with serious misconduct. Dismissal is appropriate if the charge is found to be proven – and if it's harassment, that constitutes an assault.'

'Assault?' I repeated, confused. 'Dismissal?'

Christine G— was losing patience with me. Her seat was slightly higher than mine; she was looking down at me, and the light from a high north-facing window behind her was so strong that I had to keep blinking and turning away to rest my eyes. I felt terrifically at a disadvantage, as if I were importuning her. In fact, this sense of being out of date, irrelevant, reminded me painfully of certain days when I have visited my daughter and she has gone about her business in the house as if I weren't there. So this is about middle-aged mothers and daughters, then, just as the old council members and I (with my sudden pity, my reluctance to condemn) are about fathers and middle-aged daughters. I realised that I was afraid of this young woman. I was her political mother, and she was busily, calmly, coldly demolishing me and my wimpy scruples, my desire to have mercy.

'What's going on here is fear,' she said, bizarrely seeming to read my mind. 'Fear of power being eroded and questioned. So they close ranks. This whole case has threatened the university's name, and the college's. They talk about wanting to have "excellence", but at the same time they're letting this kind of thing happen. Women don't *make up* these stories. Sexual harassment is an abuse of power.'

I began to speak about what had happened at Ormond since the Smoko. In my outline of the way the matter had been dealt with by the young women and their supporters, I used the word *ferocity*. Her face chilled and hardened further.

'I'm feeling something,' she said, still calm and polite, but icy, 'about the word you used – *ferocity*. Where you would say *ferocity*, I would say *courage*. The emphasis of the university procedures against sexual harassment is "Maybe the bloke didn't mean it". Women now are saying, "I don't care if he meant it or not – he did me harm."'

'What do you think that harm *is*?'

'It could be sexual. It could set up the teacher-student relationship on certain terms and it will always *be* on those terms.'

'It will remain on those terms,' I snapped, 'only if the woman *lets* it.'

'Yes,' she said, 'but a seventeen-year-old doesn't know how to change the terms. How can a woman who's scared of being harassed stay back to chat with her tutor? Men students can – they're not afraid. If a woman student does, she can easily start to feel that harassment is her *fault* – that she's doing something to provoke it.'

Of course these problems are real. Every woman knows it. But this constant stress on passivity and weakness – this creation of a political position based on the virtue of help-lessness – I *hate* it. I was having to hold on to my temper, as she was to hers.

'As you get older,' I said, knowing as the words left my mouth that they were the classic refrain of old to young and could only produce rebellion, 'you begin to under-stand that a lot of men in these harassment situations are *weak*. You realise that behind what you saw as force, all those years, there's actually a sort of terrible pathos. Blokes who come on to girls are putting themselves out on a limb – their *self* is at risk. You start to learn that women have got a particular power of their own, if only they knew it.'

'A girl in her first tute,' she said stubbornly, 'doesn't know that.'

'That's true – but our job as feminists is to *teach* them this, surely. To a woman of my age, blokes who behave as Colin Shepherd was accused of doing aren't scary or pow-erful. They're just poor bastards.'

She bristled. 'They may be "just poor bastards", but they've abused their power. Sexual harassment is ulti-mately not *about* sex. It's about power.' She threw the old chestnut at me with a flourish of defiance.

I said between clenched teeth, 'I don't see how you can unravel those two threads, sex and power, so neatly. They're tightly entangled. You can't *say* that – it doesn't *mean* anything.'

She shrugged. There was a long silence. We parted coolly.

As I walked down the stairs of the Union building I thought in dismay, is this what feminism has mutated into – these cold-faced, punitive girls? Or – *Is there any cause in nature that makes these hard hearts?*

~

Again and again, in trying to understand the Ormond story, I came up against a disproportionate ferocity, a stubborn desire on the part of certain feminist ideologues to paint themselves and their sisters as outraged innocents. To them there is no light end of the spectrum. They use the word *violence* in places where to me it simply does not belong.

'I think it should be criminal for a man to sexually harass a woman,' one young activist had said to me. 'Women should have the right to bring the police in, right from the start. There should no longer be two branches of response to violence against women.'

There it was again, in three short sentences – the slide from *harassment* to *violence*. 'What worries me,' I said, 'is that this rules out gradations of offence.'

'There's already a gradation,' said the girl, looking me right in the eye, but with a smiling, courteous charm. 'There's indecent assault, and there's sexual assault. That's a gradation.'

Seeing what happened to Colin Shepherd as the result of an indecent assault charge, I did not accept this as a particularly fine distinction. I outlined the Ormond case to her, and asked if she saw any disproportion in its outcome. 'But we *want* there to be consequences for men,' she said. 'These women took the formal legal channel to get redress for what's essentially unjust behaviour.'

Unjust? *Unjust* is the word for the behaviour of men

who use their position of power as a weapon in forcing women to endure their repeated sexual approaches, or who take revenge for a knockback by distorting a woman's career or making her workplace intolerable or sacking her. *Unjust* does not apply to a clumsy pass at a party by a man who's had too much to drink. The two things belong in different moral realms. But my young activist would not agree. She had a grid labelled *criminal*, and she was determined to lay it down on the broadest field of male behaviour she could get it to encompass. 'As you can see,' she said, 'I'm passionate about this.' Craziest of all, by criminalising hapless social blunders she actually believed she was 'empowering' women.

'The Catholic church,' said a Jewish woman I know, 'took centuries to achieve what these puritan feminists have managed to do in only a couple of years – take an idea whose purpose was to free people, and turn it into something that strangles truth.'

~

Is it wimpy, is it soft on men, to believe in at least trying conciliation? Sonya O—, the lawyer who was Victoria's Equal Opportunity Commissioner until the Liberal government abolished her job, certainly doesn't think so. She's in her forties, almost our scrap-heap generation, but though she is quick to laugh and has a keen sense of the absurd, her eyebrows are fierce and I can imagine her gaze, in a crisis, having the force of an oncoming truck.

'Commonsense tells you,' she said, '"For Christ's sake deal with this *immediately*!" But it's hard to achieve conciliation if you formalise it at an early stage. Most people when they're accused want to defend themselves as hard as possible. As soon as a bloke is given notice of a complaint, he gets upset and angry. He doesn't see his behaviour as untoward. He thinks there's been a "mis-representation". This is why we don't usually send the respondent a written, fully detailed account of the complaints – because it throws him into a state of anger and denial – a great rallying of forces to respond to the charge. They dig in. Usually they will deny it. They will *all* deny it. One bloke went on making credible denials, backed up by his employer, right up to the moment when we produced the semen-stained letter – then he collapsed.

'But ninety-six per cent of cases are settled and you hear nothing about them in the media. A face-saving settlement is possible, as long as there's speed, confidentiality and trust. Great efforts are made for everyone to *hear* each other. We *fight* to keep confidentiality. In a closed community it's always best if the person's peers can deal with it. There was a surgeon, for example – we got in touch with a senior colleague and said, "Fix it." Never heard another word about it. We took a hell of a risk. And it wouldn't work again, because people would say due process hadn't been observed.

'It's the eternal question: why, when you set up informal, fast processes for personal ignition points, do the processes always tend to become lumbering, vast, politically laden machines with caterpillar treads, that don't deal with the problem? If only we could zoom in, troubleshoot and zoom out – maybe with follow-up. Essentially, sexual harassment is bullying. The hardest thing for women is to stop it themselves. They need someone to hold their hand while they do it. You need an individual who can say "*Oy!*"'

I remarked that her attitudes looked benevolent compared with the new feminists' push on campus to sidestep

conciliation and go 'straight to retribution'. Sonya O—
pulled a face and looked out the window at the commer-
cial towers of Collins Street.

'If you don't take certain positions these days,' she said,
'you're "not a feminist". Dear God, if I know *anything*, I
know that there are ten thousand ways of being a feminist.'

~

People who think that degrees of assault should suffice are
impatient with what one woman lawyer described as the
fuzziness, the *murky waters* of conciliation. They call it *soft
law* and they scorn it. But conciliation, when you think
about it, is psychologically a feminine – almost a motherly
– way of settling a dispute. It rests on the idea, commonsense to any mother of warring children, that more than
one interpretation of 'the facts' can legitimately exist; on
the possibility that there has been a genuine misunderstanding – or at least a gross mismatch of expectations. It
has concern for the wounded feelings, the pride, of both
parties. It takes into account that a story told over and over
loses its tight fit with 'the truth' and becomes a story about
a story. It allows people to escape from corners they may
have painted themselves into, in their first wild burst of
defensiveness. It admits the complexities of context which
the rules of evidence in courts exclude. A certain patience
is required, however, and a basic optimism about the ability of people to learn and change. The Ormond complainants and their supporters ran out of this patience; or
perhaps they never had it. Perhaps they never believed, in
their rage and frustration, that anything other than brute
force would blast a hole through the battlements of men's

privilege. So they charged past conciliation into the traditional masculine style of problem-solving: call in the cops, split off the relevant nuances of character and context, and hire a cowboy to slug it out for you in the main street at noon, with all the citizenry watching.

~

In a café I gossiped with Angela Z—, a woman friend of my age, about our recent experiences with younger feminists. My friend had written a piece for the *Age* about the impossibility of buying attractive, comfortable shoes in large sizes; when her article was run, she received more than thirty letters from readers, some of them very funny and to the point. The male editor wouldn't agree to her writing a follow-up, and suggested she try the Accent pages. She got on to the editor of these pages and made her proposal.

'Yes, I read your piece,' said the Accent editor, a woman. 'Accent publishes feminist things. What line would you be running?'

My friend explained her idea, but the Accent editor declined, on the grounds that it was *not feminist enough*.

'If you don't think it's a feminist issue,' my friend said crossly, 'that women outside the so-called normal size range can't buy decent clothes, then I think you're wrong.'

'Why don't you offer it to the Tempo section?' said the Accent editor. '*They* run frivolous things.'

At the word *frivolous* we began to utter shrieks of coarse laughter; and then, for some reason, we recalled the older women from the suburbs who used to turn up to women's liberation meetings in the city, twenty years ago. They would sit quietly, listening to our rantings: Fima, Rose, old Jewish women with gentle smiles and bosoms, who never came to a meeting without bringing gifts of food. We gobbled it and never thought to ask them questions about their lives or why they had come; we were too selfish, too full of our own grievances and theories. I related to my friend my pathetic bravado in the presence of the fierce young Women's Officer from the Student Union. 'I practically pleaded for her respect,' I said. 'I talked about abortion law reform, demos and police and so on – I said, "We put our bodies on the line" – but she just looked at me coldly – she didn't give a shit about our *magnificent heroism*.'

We sat at the table howling with laughter. 'It's a dialogue between generations,' said Angela Z—, wiping away the tears.

'It's not a dialogue,' I said, blowing my nose. 'It's a fucking *war*.'

On a clear morning in late April I drove out to Mont Albert to visit Mr Andrew McA—, the member of the council's Group of Three who had written to me offering an interview. On the phone he had used the sarcastic expression 'your feminist mates'; I was wary. As soon as he opened the door I had a strange and not entirely pleasant sense that I had seen him somewhere before. I racked my brains to place him, while his wife settled me at a table in a room with a big mirrored sideboard and floor-to-ceiling windows that gave on to a garden. A railway line ran nearby: occasional trains caused a faint shudder.

Mr McA— took his place opposite me at the table. He looked in his seventies, dressed in neat wool pants and a viyella shirt open at the neck. He had moistened and combed his hair, but there was a rebellious little wave over his forehead which he had failed (all his life, perhaps) to subdue. He was thin, scrubbed, dry, like a Scot; he had battered hands with big, blunt thumbs. And suddenly I remembered where I had seen him. He was one of the two old Ormond men who had so forcefully asserted their claim to my seat behind the Shepherds at the County

Court appeal. I was severely thrown by this memory. I bristled with hostility: at first I could hardly meet his eye. But he obviously had no memory of me. On his private turf, Mr McA— was a different man. He still held his chin high, but the tough posture was softened by a smile and a warm expression. I didn't mention the incident, but I tried to keep the tone of his public self alive in my mind while we talked. This was made difficult by his welcome, and more so by the cheerful friendliness of his wife, who asked if she could call me by my first name, and at eleven on the dot crashed open a servery hatch from the kitchen and passed us coffee and excellent home-made cheese biscuits. She told me she had left a bag of cooking apples from their tree beside the front door for me to take home. 'Don't bite them,' she said. 'They need stewing – they're terribly sour.' 'But they fluff up very nicely,' added Mr McA—.

On the table between Mr McA— and me lay a low mountain range of files. More were spread out on the floor, and others burst out of a battered briefcase that leaned against the leg of his chair. He had letters, memos, minutes, photocopies of every conceivable relevant document. I longed for him to find pressing business elsewhere and leave me to graze on them undisturbed; but he was their captive. He would start his version of the events, then cut across himself, dive for a sheet of paper and read me a paragraph off it, then cast it aside and leap for another sheet. 'I can't place my hand on it,' he would say as he shuffled through the mound. 'It's not that these are out of order – it's just that I'm not exactly sure where it *is*.' Like me he could not find an organising principle for this mass of detail. Such powers of discrimination as either of us had were swamped.

He read to me excerpts from notes he had taken in court, stressing always the gaps in witnesses' memories, the inconsistencies in their stories. His anxiety about proof and likelihood was infectious. I became confused and started to panic.

After half an hour of this torture, Mr McA— suddenly pushed his chair back from the table and swung sideways towards the window. He folded his arms and began to speak more spontaneously, as if in a conversation where nothing had to be proved. He expressed frustration that the Group of Three had had such a narrow brief, with no power to call witnesses, no protection against defamation, no way of 'compelling people to tell the truth'. He said he was one of those who believed strongly that Peter M—, the Vice-Master, ought to have spoken at once to Dr Shepherd and told him there were 'real, active complaints around'. He spoke with dry anger against one of the college's senior women tutors who, he said, had undermined Peter M—'s early handling of the complaints and had accused him (here he extracted a letter from a file) of being 'obstructionist and sexist'. He showed me evidence that pointed persuasively to the identity of the council member who had leaked proceedings to the press. And he spoke with intense irritation about the High Court judge's prompt resignation from the chairmanship of the council. Something in his tone as he said these things made me forget for a moment that Mr McA— was probably fifteen years older than the judge: I thought with surprise, so – even to old men, judges represent the father.

We talked for a long time, trying to compare our senses

of the thing, to find a common place to stand. The differences between us in age, sex and experience of life made this almost impossible, but the attempt was genuine, and the companionableness which developed between us was strangely sad.

I went away from this meeting (and a later one) with Mr McA— weighed down by a sense of his distress and confusion. It seemed to me that his response to the events in question was so complicated by the depth of his emotional attachment to the college that he could only flounder in the oceans of detail he had amassed. I could not get a fix on his attitude. At first I thought he seemed to believe either that Dr Shepherd had done the things alleged and thus deserved to be fired, or that the two girls had made up stories out of malice or neurosis, in which case the college should have gone in to bat for Shepherd with real vigour. But his position seemed to shift repeatedly as we talked, and when I read back over my notes I found that at the outset he had said, 'Colin Shepherd has been penalised far too heavily – out of proportion.' *Was* there 'proportion', or was it a case of either/or? I think he wasn't sure. But he did stand firm on one thing: 'In my personal view,' he said, 'we should make sure that Colin Shepherd is treated fairly on being parted from. Some parties would believe in being as stingy as possible – fulfilling the minimum legal obligation – but it doesn't pay to be parsimonious. You can't have a man feeling really sore and foul about the college.'

Privately I wondered yet again at the passion certain people – usually men – harbour for institutions. I will never understand this emotion; and my inability to sympathise with it handicaps me in trying to grasp the 'truth' of this story. It is completely mysterious to me, even somewhat distasteful, that someone might fall in love with an institution *for life*, and that his loyalty to it might unsettle his broader ethical judgments.

The bag of cooking apples was on the car seat beside me as I drove away. While I waited for a traffic light to change, I thought I would try one, despite the McA—'s kind warning. I took one bite – they were right: my saliva dried up, and every hair on my head stood on end.

A woman I vaguely know. and rather like, a big hand-some laughing Catholic mother in her early fifties who has come late to feminism, related a discussion she'd had with her sister, 'that could have become an argument but didn't, about the way women in our family *flirt*. I realised it a few years back,' she said, 'and tried to stop doing it. We send out *messages*, to get a buzz back that'll make you feel good for the rest of the day – but the poor bloke's left wondering, "Now what did all *that* mean?"'

She spoke about the differences between her mother's generation and hers, about the distorting power of a Catholic upbringing about sex: 'It's education that makes the biggest change. Once you start to *read*, once you start to realise that you've been lied to about A, you start to question B, C, D and E – and then the whole house of cards collapses.'

Yes, I thought, that's a wonderful thing – but not if Eros, 'the spark that ignites and connects', gets extinguished in the wreckage. What's wrong with flirting? Perhaps it made the *men* 'feel good for the rest of the day', too. Why be so literal-minded about it? Why does it have to be harmful or wrong? Who says it has to *mean* something beyond itself? It's play. It's the little god Eros, flickering and flashing through the plod of our ordinary working lives.

Feminism is meant to free us, not to take the joy out of everything.

~

Lance Peters, whose work Margaret L— had suggested might be 'an important source' for my project, turned out to be the man who had written the screenplay of an Australian feature movie called *Gross Misconduct* which, in a stroke of breathtaking synchronicity, had been shot on location at Ormond College while aspects of the Colin Shepherd drama had been unfolding in real life. In Peters' plot, the student who brought a charge of misconduct against her lecturer was a neurotic, damaged girl, engaged in an incestuous affair with her father. She had seduced the innocent academic, a handsome family man and inspiring neo-Platonist teacher who in his spare time played funky saxophone in clubs. The movie was released in the winter of 1993, and screened for a brief period without creating a stir.

Patrick N—, a Labor man and jazz buff of fifty or so, came to live in Ormond as a tutor at Colin Shepherd's suggestion. Like many people who have known Shepherd for a long time, he spoke of him with a kind of rough, impatient affection. Patrick N— gave me the first graphic eye-witness account I had heard of the fateful Smoko in October 1991.

'The Valedictory Dinner ends the year with a bang,' he said, launching into it with gusto, 'and after that, through the exams, the rest of it's a whimper. I'm a highly emotional slob, I love it – and it's emotional for the kids, too, though they have a love-hate relationship with Ormond – more love than hate.

'The dinner is quite an occasion. Darkness, candles, a piper pipes the procession in, the Governor of Victoria was there, the staff's in academic dress, black tie is religiously observed.

'Colin Shepherd made a brief speech, then the two senior kids – a woman and a man – gave the Valedictory addresses. They were brilliant speeches. The whole show was worth going to just for them. Then they sang "Land of Hope and Glory" – that's the Ormond song. The kids sing it Cossack-style. They stand on the chairs – they're asked not to stand on the tables – let's say *some* of them don't.

'The High Table processes out, then the kids go out.

'Then the deal is you get into your old stuff and you go to the Smoko. Everyone's well on the way by the time they get there, given the highly emotional night it is – and it was made more emotional on this occasion because the Master had announced the results of the election for the chair of the Student Club – and it was a woman. She was elected against two blokes – one of them was the captain of rugby.

'People went berserk with happiness. I was one of them. She walked past me and I congratulated her – I gave her a kiss on the cheek and told her she could use my phone to ring her parents. So it was a Valedictory Dinner but with this extra tang – the election of a woman chair. Some of the blokes were saying to me later, "The place is going to the fuckin' dogs – bloody women."

'The Smoko started at about eight-thirty. Everyone was in their olds, the grog was flowing. I've got a reputation for dancing with everybody on the bloody floor. I'm a physical person and my friends warn me – that's the safety element of these things – you don't dance with just one kid. It was a great party – but it wasn't a *wild* party.

'Colin said to me three or four days after the event, "Did you enjoy yourself?" I said, "Yes, but I'm disgusted with myself. I spewed, first time in thirty-five years." Colin said, "I got a bit full myself." And he gave a little nervous laugh.

'Now the cruel, cruel irony is that I didn't believe him. I thought, oh, it's just Colin trying to be one of the boys.

I thought, come off it, Colin, you never drop your guard. Well, Colin hasn't really got a guard, but – in twenty years of social occasions at the Monash faculty I'd never seen him drunk.'

I asked him if he had any sense that Colin Shepherd had been in over his head, in the Master's job. He looked amazed, and answered warmly.

'*God*, no! He was a *marvellous* Master. He might have been a bit too paternalistic, too avuncular – but in my judgement of Colin, this job was the pinnacle of everything he'd ever wanted. When Francis Ormond built that college, he had someone like Colin Shepherd in mind. Colin loves pomp, he loves circumstance, he loves connections with the church. Also, one thing he's very good at is meetings. His interventions are astute, sensible, timely, and always well expressed. He thinks very well on his feet. He speaks well. And the kids were so bloody pleased that he was the first Australian Master.'

When I mentioned the High Court judge, whose role was cut short so sharply by his resignation from the college council, Patrick N— burst into scornful laughter. 'He's the metaphor for Colin's tragedy. A knight, ex-Ormond, a man with all the right connections. Before his troubles, Colin would be saying to you, "Come and meet His Honour" – then at the first hiccup – see ya later. It's the supreme tragedy of Colin Shepherd – that the establishment he devoted his bloody life to has turned round and kicked him to death.'

~

One curious detail kept surfacing, in the many accounts I heard of the Smoko in question: a woman who took off her top in the Junior Common Room and danced bare-breasted.

The first man who reported it to me described it bluntly as 'clearly not a sexual act. It was "I am a woman and a woman's been elected". It was obviously a *political* act.' As a veteran of the feminist social milieux of the seventies, I didn't find this outrageous or even particularly strange. In fact it struck me as spirited and flamboyant, if somewhat rash. I simply made a note of it and passed on. But the little story kept popping up. I was not permitted to forget it. What was its status as testimony? Rumour, gossip, fact? I didn't know how to evaluate it, or what it meant. But up it came of its own accord, like an urban myth, over and over, from almost every quarter, whether hostile to the complainants or friendly, whenever college people spoke to me about the Smoko. I never brought it up: it was always offered to me, laid down on the table in front of me like a mysterious tarot card. Those who claimed to have seen the bare-breasted dancer with their own eyes would present the story coolly, without making anything of it, as if merely adding atmosphere to their account of the evening. Others who had only heard it round the traps tended to raise it as if it proved something, although exactly what I could not determine.

I had a friend in Ormond, to whom I reported the rumour. At first he refused to believe it. Then, as I came back again and again with it, he stuck doggedly to his guns. 'No no *no*. I do *not* believe it. It can't be true. Perhaps someone was just dancing about triumphantly – perhaps she *looked* topless. Perhaps someone who was really drunk thought they saw someone topless in the distance, and told somebody else about it. It must be a collective hallucination. You've got to realise that colleges are extraordinary hotbeds of the most circumstantial gossip.' After about the seventh reported sighting he was still obstinately maintaining denial. At the tenth resurgence he began to waver. He said, in the tone of somebody lost in realms of cloudy fantasy, 'Well . . . I suppose that nearly everyone there that night was blind drunk . . . if it *did* happen, it suggests some sort of . . . *Walpurgisnacht*.'

But what fascinated and amused me most about this resilient little factoid was that the older the man who was discussing it with me, the more rapidly he would skid from plain statement into lurid embroidery. 'Danced topless' would become 'danced topless *on a table*', then 'danced *naked* on a table', then 'danced *newd* on a table'. Each time I witnessed this slither into prurience, it was completely unconscious. When I drew the speaker's attention to his slip, his face would go blank with surprise and embarrassment. So a gesture (however foolish, in this context) intended as symbolic of female glee, or celebration and triumph, is transformed by the older men who speak of it into something sleazy – an act of gross sexual provocation, with overtones of prostitution. They can't help it. *They don't even know they're doing it.* There must be something useful we can learn from this.

What sort of a night *was* it, Wednesday 16 October 1991? That depends, of course, on who is remembering.

It *was spring. Exams* were coming. It was *a splendid occasion, a triumphant event, a very successful function.* During a speech at dinner *people were screaming through the vents.* It was *just another college evening. Nothing to distinguish* it from *any other Smoko. From memory* it was *a warmish night. A nice night* to *stay around* after dinner and have *a few drinks.* But some people *thought, no,* and *went home.* A woman *visiting from another college* said to the Master *Let's go and see what the kids are doing.* It was *a strange night.* There was *definitely something in the air. A loss of authority. A lot* of the *tutors* were *drunk, dancing with each other, pinching* people's *bums. Let's go and see what the kids are doing.* One of the *senior* tutors was *blotto.* She *took an earring* out of *her ear* – it was *a pink, reasonably large ball* – and *gave it* to a boy. There was *a sense of abandon.* One *woman* took her *top off.* There wasn't *a good feel* about the night. People who *hate Smokos* were *not in euphoria.* People were *very drunk* so *don't count on subtleties* but they *heard stories.* The room was *dark;* the *only light* came in from the quadrangle. It was *a great* party but not a *wild* party. *See what the kids are doing.* They asked him *to dance.* Maybe there was *an element of teasing.* Perhaps *at first* it was *almost a kind of game. At least one* person was *dazed and confused.* It was *a warmish night.* Something *in the air. Let's go and see what the kids are doing.*

But the Bureau of Meteorology recorded that on Wednesday 16 October 1991 in Melbourne there were 'showers and rain. The top temperature was 14.6°, winds were moderate from the south-west; it was fine in the evening.' Of this at least we can be certain.

~

On 28 April 1993 the papers reported that a fourteen-year-old girl on her way to school had been raped in a public toilet by a man armed with a knife. This is the kind of news item that makes women call each other on the phone. I thought, contemplating it, that our helpless rage and grief at this eternally unpreventable violence against women and girls – our inability to protect our children from the sickness of the world – must get bottled up and then let loose on poor blunderers who get drunk at parties and make clumsy passes; who skate blithely into situations that they are too ignorant or preoccupied to recognise as minefields of gender politics. But the ability to discriminate *must be maintained.* Otherwise all we are doing is increasing the injustice of the world.

It was the end of April 1993, but the days were still warm and dry, and the hoses were going in the Ormond gardens, when I went there to interview Fergus C—, a tutor who didn't look much older than his mid-thirties but displayed the articulate, unshakeable self-assurance that is the mark of the Ormond man. He welcomed me at the gate and took me on a little tour of the place, starting with the Master's office which had so recently been Colin Shepherd's. We stood at the door and peered in. In the middle of the floor stood a brightly painted child's table and chairs; he told me these had been made by some Ormond students and entered in a competition: they hadn't won, but the Acting Master, who had a small child, had made an offer for them. They struck an oddly homely note in the formal office with its towering ceiling and immense, high windows. Fergus C— took a few steps towards the great timber desk, looked at me with a naughty smile, spread his arms, and said, 'Well, Helen – this is the scene of the crime!'

I stared around the room.

'There's the door,' he said, pointing towards the one that led out into the passage, 'and this is the key' – he flourished it between thumb and forefinger – 'that poor Colin Shepherd had to hold up in court.'

The key was heavy, curly, very old, like something out of a fairy tale. I glanced again at the door and saw its Victorian style, its low keyhole and handle. 'Oh!' I said. 'I'd imagined a more modern one – that could be just flicked shut.'

'No,' he said. 'It's quite hard to turn. That's a point Colin tried to make in court.'

Taken aback by his cheerful, dramatic frankness, I scanned the room. I saw the sideboard, the two low puffy chairs with their wooden arms, side by side; suddenly the scene came to life for me. The ghosts materialised. A middle-aged man fumbled in his elation with the whisky decanter and filled two glasses, slopping a few drops on to the glossy surface of the timber. A gorgeous young woman, flushed from dancing, a blur of beauty, sat and glowed in the chair. *And then what happened?* What was the truth? It was unknowable. I looked for the windows – could anyone have glanced in and seen them? No – the sills were shoulder-high. For some reason I felt a rush of terrible sadness. Young Fergus suggested we conduct the interview out in the garden, and I followed him out of the room with relief, to a bench that was shaded by trees but out of reach of the big leisurely hoses.

'Colin, by style and temperament,' he said, 'will always collide with the politically correct gang who've had a foot in Ormond since Davis McCaughey brought a liberal cast of mind into a patriarchal set-up, twenty years ago almost to the day. Colin's not *of* the establishment, but his whole life has been directed towards it, and he had links with it that would have been useful to the college. He had a track record with young people. And he was *indefatigable*. He seems not to sleep. I've seen the files from his time in the job – it's amazing, the amount of stuff he pumped out. He was having a ball in the job.

'It was the end of his first full year as Master. Alcohol was flowing. He had entertained the Governor. It was a case of hubris, of forgetting to be careful. He exposed his flank, and he was ruthlessly attacked.

'He's an *innocent* man. There's a lot of good in him. A disproportionate reaction strikes me, in this. My account-ant's a woman. When she heard about the case, that it was an accusation of groping, she said to me, "*What*? You mean that's *it*?" One of the senior women in college rightly asked, at a council meeting, "What level of conduct is required of the Master of Ormond College?" – but there's always been bad blood between her and Colin Shepherd.

'The Master is a representative figure. He's the face of the patriarchy, of the institution. As with royalty, there's no allowance for a lapse – no concept of a venial sin. And Colin was unaware of the sensitivity of his position. He doesn't tune in.

'I don't think he's ever panicked. There's a strength of purpose, a will in him that I'd never have suspected. You could look him in the eye and he wouldn't bat an eyelid. He sailed right along. His wife has gone through the behavioural changes you'd have expected in *him*.

'You or I might talk about something like "develop-ments in contemporary feminism" – neither of them would know what you meant. They're unworldly. I'd repeat the word *innocent*. A lack of perception. *Something* was going to happen. It wasn't a surprise to me.

'But why has the world seized on it?' he went on,

changing smoothly into rhetorical mode. 'The women who support the complainants see the university as an island of purity in a corrupt sea. Ormond represents offensiveness butting in. Despite its multi-cultural pretences, our society is still very British. This story is a volatile mix of the establishment and sex. The media finds nothing more entertaining than that. If you *live* here, on the one hand you're appalled by the publicity – but on the other you realise that perhaps it means that Ormond *matters*.'

He pulled out of his briefcase a folder of colour photos and spread them out between us on the wooden bench, rummaging through them for the one he wanted me to see. As he searched I picked one at random. It showed Colin Shepherd on green grass, strolling towards the camera with his hands in his pockets. He was wearing a football jumper in Ormond stripes, and a battered bush hat. His head was turned to his right, towards the backs of a line of young men who seemed to be engrossed in watching a football match. The placing of the figures in the photo, the directions in which they were facing, created a strong sense of melancholy and exclusion.

'Here it is,' said Fergus. He passed me another photo. 'It's the Master's Dance. Normally the Master would turn up in black tie.' It was a full-length shot of Dr and Mrs Shepherd standing arm in arm in a living room, looking straight into the lens. Dr Shepherd's face was serious, his wife's about to break into a diffident smile. He was wearing an eighteenth-century soldier's uniform with breeches, plus a blond curly wig and a tricorne hat, and Mrs Shepherd a purple, flounced, big-sleeved Victorian gown.

'See?' said Fergus. 'They just didn't *get* it.'

The photos, with their touching human note, brought

me up short; but Fergus C— was such a vivid, fluent talker, so intelligent and young and entertaining, so proud of his college, that I was hardly aware of the gradual chilling of my blood; and it wasn't till I typed up my notes that I noticed the merciless closing-out of the Shepherds from possible college society that I had just witnessed.

~

This sharp sense of style was common to every member of the Ormond community who spoke to me, student or teacher, past or present. Some students struggled to extract moral meaning from it, others gloried in it, others again just wielded it, with varying degrees of irony and self-awareness.

'I came from a state school,' said one young man, now a lawyer, a tall, freckled blond in a grey suit and a raincoat. 'I'd had jobs since I was twelve, and I thought Ormond would be full of "spoilt" private school kids. But when I got there I found they had skills I just didn't have. They were socially very advanced, good at talking to people. They knew what clothes to wear, whereas at Smokos, for example, I tended to overdress. I saw after a while that there was a college uniform: Blundstone boots, denim jeans, a black T-shirt, and those check flannel shirts that the engineers wore. I realised it was anathema to draw attention to yourself. If you're rich, the worst thing you can do is let people know. If you're intelligent, you don't draw attention to it. The look to have was one of self-effacement – of not making any attempt. You don't care. What could be cooler than that?'

'At first,' said a young woman graduate who was still looking for a job, 'it's like a big holiday camp – so grownup, so sophisticated. People are spastic for the whole of Orientation Week, and by the end of it a hierarchy is established – the in people, and the dags. The first few weeks I was at the pub with the glamour girls, the "gorgeous pretty girlies"' – her face positively rippled with disdain – 'then I became known as a feminist, and halfway through the year I was dropped.'

As she spoke, very open-faced and smiling, she kept flipping her long silk hair back over one shoulder. 'I was told that no man would come near me with a ten-foot pole, because I was so aggressive.'

'Some people, like Nicky Stewart for example,' said a science graduate who was working in another country and phoned me from there with her views, 'thought O-Week was cruel – sexist and nasty. But at Ormond there are high school kids, and kids from Scotch and Geelong College and Morongo – they sit at the table asking each other "What did *you* get in HSC?" If you don't treat them badly, give them some harmless violence and a bit of pain to talk about at breakfast, they'll never mix.'

'I only stayed in Ormond a year,' said a history graduate, a self-possessed young woman from the country who had joined the college choir halfway through the year after she moved out. 'The tradition didn't work on me. I thought it was silly. I hated the heirarchical thing – Gentlemen and SCUM, meaning Student Club Uninitiated Member – all that stuff. You were yelled at in O-Week, they threw water bombs, you were told to do tapskulls – drink beer straight from the tap, to see how much you could take. They took us all to a beach and we were supposed to do this stuff called Sexercises. Blokes lay on their backs in a line and rolled a woman along their raised hands. Push-up competitions. I didn't think it was funny. I went to the beach, but I just walked off and sat down with the "gentlemen", the female ones.' She gave an ironic laugh. 'I had feelings at the time which I didn't really understand till after I'd done Women's Studies. I didn't like all that Ormond-importance stuff, the songs putting down other colleges' – she clenched her fists and pounded the table in a sharp rhythm. 'I'd already lived away from home, and I didn't want to get pissed all the time. Basically I just lived in my room, in a rather isolated section of the college.'

'There's an aura to the place,' said a graduate now working as an engineer, a dry-mannered, soft-faced young man, still dressed in what the lawyer had described as 'the college uniform'. 'The buildings reek of tradition. I like them. It's sickening, once you leave – but when you're into it you look at the day students and think, I bet they wish they were like me. The problem is that it's a discrete social unit. There's no contact with the outside world. But it's not a bad treadmill to be on. I wouldn't be surprised if I married someone I'd met through college. You can't hate a place where you made eighty per cent of your friends.'

~

'David Parker was Master when I got there,' said the lawyer. 'He was a very intimidating figure.'

'His office,' said another young man, 'was silent and calm, like a scene from a film. He'd say something to you about your parents.'

'I didn't think much of him as Master,' said the history graduate. 'He was awkward – not a people person, like Colin Shepherd. The first time I met Parker, he heard my name and said there'd been a couple of boys with that name in Ormond who were good footballers – they were a fine-looking lot, and was I any good at football?' She laughed. 'I was taken aback.'

'I was sitting at a table one day,' said the lawyer, 'and Parker came up and spoke to me. "Are you from Ballarat?" "Yes, Master." (He wanted to be addressed as Master.) "College or Grammar?" "Ballarat High."' Here the lawyer hung his head to mime shame, but he was grinning.

An arts graduate, lightly built and with a flop of brown curls, told me, from behind the cash register of the city bookshop where he worked, about a time when he and some of his friends were horsing around in the Ormond hallways with a trolley, which they crashed against the wall of a tutor's flat: the impact almost knocked over a bookcase on the other side of the wall, near which the tutor's baby had been sleeping. The tutor (by coincidence Barbara W—, the women's supporter who had shouted at me over the phone, and whom this student greatly admired) 'was terribly angry. She wanted us to be kicked out of college, but Parker said it was only boyish fun. She didn't speak to us for two years. We deserved it. We were little Country Road dicks. It's hard to dissociate yourself from the cretin that you were.'

~

'At an ordinary Smoko, not the Valedictory one,' said the engineering graduate, 'you got a stamp on your wrist when you paid your five bucks to go in. It said FUGBAS. *Fire up, get blind and score.* I'm not the predatory type,' he added, flashing a glance at my notebook. 'The girls are definitely into it – it's fun.'

'Boys didn't force themselves on you,' said the science graduate with brisk scorn. 'They waited till you were totally inebriated and *then* they slept with you. One country rugby-head went downstairs and got all his friends to come up to his room and have a look at a naked girl, who'd passed out in his bed.'

~

When I asked the lawyer what he had gained from his time in college, he replied at once, 'A complete contempt for property. We used to have fire extinguisher fights. We used to smash windows and break down doors. We trashed rooms. There was also a reasonable amount of nudity. I heard that once, after the rugby, blokes ran naked through the debating final. If we were walking to the pub, we'd just piss while we were walking along. We used to chuck bags of piss at people, at the car rallies. We had food fights. I remember one, when the food had been fish and chips. There was food everywhere, you couldn't walk on the floor, it was so sticky. The Master said, "The Hall's been raped – you promised me this wouldn't happen." It was a completely liberating sense of not caring, of being free from social control. You feel special, going to Ormond – you learn that things don't matter.'

In the middle of my distaste, which I was trying hard to conceal, a small memory wriggled to the surface: the water fights I used to have in my twenties with my first husband (an 'Ormond man', now I come to think of it, though not the nostalgic type) and the other residents of the old house we rented in Fitzroy. I remembered one fight which raged all through a winter afternoon, at the end of which, exhausted from running and throwing and laughing, I retreated to the outside dunny and sat on it, to hide and rest; but within minutes the door was wrenched open and my husband, with a demonic cackle, hurled a whole bucket of cold water all over me where I sat, panting and off my guard. I remembered being amazed by his tenacity – his refusal to *stop*.

'There's a sort of euphoria in those fights,' the lawyer was saying. 'All your muscles go weak, from the laughing.'

~

'Davis McCaughey,' a tutor remarked to me rhetorically, in a different context, 'was a brilliant Master. He'd sort of let the kids burn the place down, but they still used to quail before him. He seemed to get the balance exactly right.'

~

'I don't know what happened to the place between Mc-Caughey and Shepherd,' said a woman lawyer who had been a fresher in the seventies, in the second year after the admission of women residents – a 'very good time' for her. 'I was amazed to hear, in the late eighties, stories about raids on students' rooms, and trashings – women being afraid to walk through the halls at night. If these stories were true, it had got much uglier than when *I* was a student.'

~

'There was a huge fanfare,' the male lawyer who'd gone to school in Ballarat continued, 'when Colin Shepherd took on the job. He was the first Australian. They rang the bell seven times to show he was the seventh Master. At his first big dinner he was piped and spooned into Hall. It was a big night. Three hundred people, black-and-white, candles. I had to carve a turkey. We all got pissed, smashed glasses. People got up on the tables and sang "Land of Hope and Glory". There was a toast to the Queen. The difference between D. H. Parker and Colin Shepherd,' he went on, 'was stark. One day I was in the vestibule and I met Shepherd's eye – and he *nodded*. I was impressed. With Parker, you wouldn't have expected him to have loose eyes. I thought, Shepherd's an open guy – he's accessible.'

'I thought he should be more removed,' said the unemployed woman graduate; 'a figure of respect. He tried to get down to the students' level. I felt that this job was too much for him – that he would bumble his way through – at any minute he might muck it up. I had a sense of impending doom. If he'd been *dashing* – but I felt he was out of his depth.'

'When he invited guests to Hall,' the lawyer said, 'he would always introduce them to the students as noble, esteemed persons, a professor from India and so on. The rugby blokes in particular thought it showed bad taste – that it was demeaning of himself and of the college.'

~

Another ex-Ormond student, who was grateful to the college for having taken him in 'at a great, dangerous corner' of his life, and whose sympathy for Dr Shepherd had brought him social ostracism (one Ormond girl described him to me contemptuously as 'a friendless geek') devised a more complex analysis of the embarrassment Shepherd's public persona provoked among the style police of the student body. 'He's bloody naïve,' he said. 'A teddy bear. He had no idea how nasty people could be towards him. People were just waiting for him to fuck up. He's a deeply establishment person, a middle-of-the-road Liberal voter. He's much more personable than Parker was – but he irritated people, because he confronted us with the establishment class culture we'd inherited and were benefiting from. Where campus politics is concerned, being in Ormond, or in college at all, is pretty incorrect. Ormond students are aware that they're on the wrong side politically, so they look for other ways to marginalise themselves. For some, this is radical feminism, for others it's being gay, or Asian. They define their whole lives not by the benefits of the college, but by what oppresses them. And Colin Shepherd confronted them with the truth of the matter. At High Table he'd say, "Tonight we've got Sir and Lady So-and-So." We'd cringe. But in thirty years these same students will *be* the Sir and Lady So-and-So's. The women who brought the complaints are law students. They characterised themselves as helpless. Wait a few years. They'll be screwing companies in court.'

'I've been out in the workforce for a while,' said the engineer. 'There's constant innuendo to the secretaries – blatant sexism – much worse than what used to happen in college and at uni. The college was so much more liberal a place than the whole CBD for a start – than the real world. The university is the place where society draws its progressive ideas from – but it's not where the worst problems are.'

~

'I've been told,' said the lawyer from Ballarat, 'that the two girls will have a lot of career problems because of what they did.'

'I met Elizabeth Rosen in a nightclub,' said the bookseller, 'the night before the trial. I got a strong sense of her sincerity. It changed my whole opinion of the thing. It's not framed in terms of injury. The issue is what happens when you complain – how you're treated. The forces are so unseen – the cultural machinery they had to fight through, the opposition they came up against – why *should* they? I'd support anything the girls did. You think Ormond's a benign, safe world, until something like this happens. The Master's a victim, but a powerful victim.'

'I liked Nicky Stewart a lot,' said the lawyer. 'I thought she was attractive and gutsy. She doesn't know my name. Elizabeth Rosen is a really smart girl. But I don't feel comfortable, talking about her.' He gave a grimace of a smile, dropped his eyes and twisted his shoulders. Sensing personal emotion, I backed off; but I wondered, as I had many times before, whether Elizabeth Rosen had any real awareness of the profound effect she has on men.

'Nicole Stewart,' said the unemployed graduate, 'was two years older than me. I had a lot of respect for her. She dressed differently. At one ball I remember she was wearing a hat. She was a great, gutsy woman. She would stand up in Students' Club meetings and say, "You *stupid* men." Elizabeth Rosen I had no respect for. I used to live opposite her in first year. She never went to uni. She played loud music very late. She never went to meals, never seemed to eat a thing. She had a big bust but she was thin around the hips. She wasn't anorexic – she just saw no value in eating.'

'Nicky Stewart never fitted in,' said the science graduate who called collect from America. 'She wasn't a private school kid. She didn't care for the yuppie life and way of doing things – the social life. With her it was "I'm an intellectual". Elizabeth was more "Ha-de-ha, I've got more money than I know what to do with". So it was two college misfits who went ahead with complaints.'

~

'You know the dresses the girls wear to these formal do's?' said an older Ormond resident. 'They're all'– he made sinuous narrowing, then overflowing gestures with both hands – '*got up*, like chocolates about to be opened. That's the male point of view on it, anyway.'

'Once I went to the Ormond ball,' said the history graduate. 'It was held that year at the Metro nightclub – awful place, I hated it. I wore a short black skirt and high heels – and I was amazed at the way blokes I'd seen round Ormond all year suddenly started behaving towards me in a different way. Afterwards I threw out the clothes. It's not that I don't want to be seen as attractive or sexy. It's more that I don't want that response from people *I* don't want to appeal to. Some women – I don't understand it but they seem not to feel *worthy* unless they're being treated that way. I found I could always deal with the sexism at Ormond. I dress so as to be treated the way I *want* to be treated.'

~

'I looked forward to seeing Shepherd get up in court,' said the woman graduate who was looking for work. 'I hoped and prayed they would find him guilty. I've heard the argument, from a boy whose opinion I respect, that what Shepherd was accused of doing is what every boy in college does. No one says it's wrong when *they* do it – some girls even *like* it.'

One of the senior college tutors told me that recently, at a dinner to celebrate the grand centenary of the Dining Hall and to raise bursary money, 'a tutor asked a student to sit on his lap – at the *table*. If I'd been that girl, I'd have seen that as sexual harassment, but she didn't seem to mind. And afterwards, when I asked people who'd been at the table what they'd thought of it, they all said, "What?" They hadn't even noticed it.'

'But boys are stupid when they're young,' the unemployed graduate went on. 'With the position of Master, its privileges, you have to accept the responsibility – and with that comes the acceptance that people will judge you more severely than others. But maybe a crime should be a crime, regardless of age?' Here she paused and frowned, trying to get a grip on the slippery morals of the thing. 'The law *isn't* fair. More *is* expected of him.' Now she felt herself back on firmer ground. 'Yes. He's supposed to be a pillar of the community. If *he* gets away with it, what hope have we got? And I was disgusted by the age difference.'

A little jet from the unconscious showed in her use of the word *disgusted*. Why should 'the age difference' be disgusting? The violation of the incest taboo is the public obsession of our age. An anxiety has been triggered here: something dark about fathers and daughters. But she galloped on, censorious and unawares.

~

'There's a lot of young people in my position,' said the engineer, 'with a lack of passion about wrongness. I feel' – he laid his flat hand on his stomach – 'that his punishment doesn't fit the crime. His career's destroyed. I can see how it's bad but I feel sorry for him. It all went horribly wrong. The media picture of college is melodramatic. I feel like saying on the front page of the paper, "Trust me, public – it's not that impressive".'

'It seems so tragic,' said the bookseller. 'Everyone can push their trolley through it but it was an accident.'

'I used to have a moral code,' said the lawyer. 'But I realised it was useless. We're all pathetic weak human beings. I'm just a kid of twenty-two. I can't set up a code to judge a thing like this.'

~

What does it mean, then, in a place like Ormond, to manifest the wrong style? You encourage students to use your first name, instead of addressing you as Master: you *lose authority*. In the vestibule of the dining hall you nod to a student: you have *loose eyes*. You wear Hush Puppies: *the wrong kind of shoes for the Master of Ormond College*. At the end of term you help departing students by carrying their rubbish bags: you *demean yourself*. Colin Shepherd's obliviousness to the Ormond view of appropriate conduct is a measure of his vulnerability. Perhaps, if he'd been *dashing*, the word one female student used, he might have weathered it: the judge might not have *shown a clean pair of heels*; the council might have gone to the wire for him. Maybe when the girls made their complaints they were unwittingly putting a weapon in a hand not yet flexed to seize it. Maybe it was through the chink of his less-than-patrician style that the blade, whoever was holding the handle, slid in. And yet one of these students, who had been speaking about Dr Shepherd in severe terms, then struggling to make sense of his mixed feelings, suddenly turned to me and said in a rush of sympathy, 'Oh, poor Master! Are you going to be good to him?'

~

On 5 May 1993 I received a curt, three-line reply from Margaret L—, one of the women's supporters, to my scrubbed letter of the month before. She made pointed mention of her lawyer and, hammering in a fresh set of quotation marks, declined my invitation to discuss what I had called her 'version of events at Ormond College'. Once again I felt the roll of frustrated ego – but oh, how pathetic her refusals seemed, with their tight tone, their scurrying to law.

By the time I visited Mrs Shepherd it was late in the winter of 1993; the family had moved out of the Lodge months before, and back to their own house in East Malvern. I drove out there one evening, when as it happened Dr Shepherd was not at home; a friend had taken him to Barwon Heads to play golf.

Mrs Shepherd opened the front door. She was tall, with smooth cheeks, clear, dark blue eyes, and dark hair that was starting to go grey, loosely pinned up and falling in strands to her shoulders. She looked slimmer, less youthful than in the photo I had been shown by Fergus C—. Her expression, as she greeted me, was tense to the point of anguish, but she tried hard to be welcoming, and ushered me into the living room, where her two younger children, the ones I had met the year before at the Lodge, were doing their homework on the carpet next to a vigorously burning fire. Mrs Shepherd spoke gently to them and they sprang up at once and left the room.

It was a pleasant room, with three plump sofas arranged in a U facing the fire, an old blackish upright piano in one corner, and on the wall behind the couch I sat on, half a dozen undistinguished watercolours of Corpus Christi

College, mementos of the Shepherd family's happy year at Cambridge before they moved to Ormond. The chimney drew hard; several times during my visit Mrs Shepherd had to replenish the fire with logs. She sat on the carpet in front of me, in a girlish posture with her back very straight and her legs folded, and began almost immediately to cry. She hardly stopped for the whole two hours I spent with her. She held a bundle of tissues in one hand and repeatedly blew her nose and wiped her eyes. She apologised for this from the start, as if she feared that I wouldn't be able to bear the depth of her distress. She told me that she managed to hold herself together when she was with her husband and children. She didn't want him to see her like this – it would upset him so much; he needed to keep his confidence up, in the search for another job.

'I'm in grief,' she said. 'It's been totally – *surreal*. If you know you've done something, you can bear it – but when he heard that there were accusations against him, he kept saying to me, "What have I done?" If you'd asked me to list two thousand things that could happen to Colin, I wouldn't have guessed this. It's the *constancy* of the negative response to him – something about him seems to have inspired terrible hatred. It must be an urge to kill someone in authority – but I've never seen the Master of a residential college as a very important job. It's a nice position, with lots of fun, but otherwise –

'Our ears have been burning for fifteen months. If I saw one of the women's supporters when I was out walking with the children, she would turn away – you know, the snub. Sometimes we laugh – but you need a few drinks to see it as funny – two silly little people. But I *do* begrudge that he won't have a pleasant end to his life.

'When he took on the Ormond job he saw élitism, and drinking. He felt that people who came to Ormond had a responsibility to give something back, instead of just take, take, take. He invited interesting people and introduced them to the kids – to broaden them.

'Colin's ridiculously domesticated. He's the sort of person who'd be cooking a curry for dinner, and rushing out to finish mowing the lawn, and ringing up an old lady who's ill to see if she's all right. He's always thinking up ways to delight people.

'The establishment won't touch him. They're too scared. Of the feminists. He's not proud. You name it, he applies for it. I can't bear to think of him not finding a job – we'll all go crazy.'

I used the word *fate*.

'I always felt you made your *own* fate,' she said, with a fresh flood of tears. 'But it's terrible to feel so *powerless*. No matter what he did, it made no difference whatsoever. Every time the story rears its head in the press, I die again. Other people become frightened, when they think of us. We've got a friend, a teacher – he's got a Chinese student, who came to see him about some problems with her work. She entered his office looking calm. They had a distressing talk about her academic progress, and she left dishevelled. He rang Colin and said, "She could have accused me of *anything*."

'Deep down, under this extraordinary pain I feel, there's a sense of the *triviality* of this destruction.'

She wept and wept. I sat there helplessly. I said, 'Maybe

when these girls are fifty they'll look back at this and think, "What was all *that* about?"'

'I'd hope they'd have died of shame,' she said fiercely. 'Someone sent us anonymously that cutting – about one of them using the stress she'd suffered as a defence on a drink-driving charge. I thought, if *she* was drinking because she was traumatised, *I* should be drunk! Our whole family should be strung up on a *rope*!'

'The council botched it. They took fright. Their heads were in the sand. To do what they did to him was a cowardly act. I would have loved Colin to struggle on with Equal Opportunity. But it was never "*equal* opportunity". Colin was never "*equal*". They kept talking about "the victim" – *who* was the victim? I don't believe there ever was justice. But why should we claim there *should* be justice? Just look at world events!

'To deal with this is an insult to my nature. The basic assumption in the Magistrates' Court, that any man given half a chance will molest a woman, is insulting to men – it's insulting to my Colin. I can*not* understand it. None of the theories explains it. No woman could be luckier than I've been. I know he'd die rather than betray me.'

During our conversation her eldest son, whom I'd seen with his parents at the County Court, came in with a tray of tea and a banana cake that Mrs Shepherd had made and iced. She cut me a slice, but didn't take one for herself. She laughed, between sobs: 'Normally I'm a large, greedy woman.' Her son, upset to see her crying, crouched down beside her on the floor and awkwardly put his arm round her shoulder. She tried to pull herself together. 'I'm all right!' she said brightly, 'really I am!' But he left the room reluctantly, looking back at her over his shoulder.

When I left, she came to the front door with me and onto the verandah in the dark. I put out my hand and she took it in both of hers. I seem to recall that she kissed me goodbye; but even if she didn't, that's the kind of woman she is – spontaneous and sweet. I stepped off the verandah and suddenly, as I was about to walk away, she drew herself together with a visible effort and resumed a formal demeanour. She called after me a question about my book, as a piece of work in *my* life; she actually asked me *how it was going*. I stammered that I didn't know how I was going to write it. She made a flustered, brushing movement with one hand, and sang out, 'Don't worry about *me*! Just write it for *you* – don't be worried about *me*.'

For days afterwards I couldn't stop thinking about the fire in the Shepherds' sitting room. The fireplace was handsome, but it was badly designed, with an updraft that caused a tremendous burning rate and consumed a huge quantity of fuel without throwing out a commensurate amount of heat: it was always demanding to be fed. It seemed to me an image of Mrs Shepherd's generosity: her uneconomical, exhausting, undiscriminating, selfless goodwill. She told me that she had lost her faith over this; but it's rare to meet somebody whose habit is to do what the prayer book recommends: 'to give and not to count the cost'.

N ow comes a gap in the story.
       It was once filled by an interview with a man
called Professor J—, whose name had been mentioned to
me in casual conversation as someone with strong views
on what had been happening in the college. When I arrived
at his house for our appointment, he was so eager to talk
that he had already launched himself before he remembered to check my credentials and my intentions: he
seemed to be dying to tell me the story.

He sat hunched in a battered armchair, with his fists
clenched and his knees clamped together, and spoke with
bitter, trembling anger against Dr Shepherd. He had, he
said, the greatest respect for the women's supporters. He
told me that they had given the young women wise advice,
and hours of support; that they had behaved *with the highest
integrity*, and for this they had been shouted at and vilified
by the supporters of the Master and certain members of
the council. This, he said, had caused them to suffer an
immense amount of pain, anxiety and turmoil. His voice
as he spoke of these matters lost its primness and became
warm with passion. He was filled with shame and distress
at the way the council and the college had treated the girls.

It particularly grieved him that this could have happened *in a Christian college*.

After we had spoken for an hour or so, Professor J—— had to go and teach a class. I had told him about my letter to Dr Shepherd and my failed attempts to get in touch with the complainants; on his way out the door he offered to speak to Nicole Stewart and Elizabeth Rosen on my behalf. He gave me the phone number and address of his daughter who, he said, was a friend of the two women. In his garden we shook hands.

I was very troubled by what he had told me. I had an urge to ring the women's supporters who had shouted at me and written me angry letters – to say I was sorry (*for what?*) – to make another soft approach to them. I wanted to say, 'Why wouldn't *you* tell me all this? Why won't you sit down and *argue* it with me – why won't you *persuade* me?' But I thought this was only a sentimental fantasy. I believed it would be fruitless. I dreaded the fury of their response. So I never made the call.

At the same time I was naïve enough to be excited by the possibility that a path might open between me and the young women that didn't pass through the supporters' territory. I phoned Professor J——'s daughter where she worked. She was out. I left her a message. And, just to be absolutely sure, I wrote her a letter as well.

~

Dr Q——, a senior lecturer in a humanities department at Melbourne University, told me that one of his post-graduate tutors had been a student at Ormond and was 'very close to the events, though not one of the complain-ants, and is very much against Colin Shepherd. She's a terrific young woman, but she puts me in a rather awkward position – she's always bounding up to me and throwing her arm round me, and teasing me.' He laughed and looked out the window. 'I'm constantly aware that if I did likewise I'd probably be up on a charge.'

I gave him my phone number and he promised to pass it on. But the very next day this small hope collapsed. Another ex-Ormond student phoned me to arrange an interview, and mentioned in passing that the post-graduate tutor was a close friend of Ruth V—, one of the women's supporters, and used to babysit for her. I crossed the tutor off my list, and waited for the ricochet.

~

As the autumn rolled on and I imagined I was getting closer to the complainants, to the closed-off core of the matter, I began to be more scared before each interview. I developed a compulsion to arrive fanatically early, afraid that the person, irritated by a moment's lateness, would slam the door in my face. Thus I often wound up with a good half-hour to cool my heels. During these waits I would sense an unpleasant pressure, coming from some anxiety-centre inside me, to arrive with an efficiently prepared list of questions, instead of simply opening up the topic and letting the talk roll. I recognised this panic. It was the old fear of professors and people with Ph.Ds, a leftover from my own undistinguished and almost totally silent university career, thirty years ago.

But I was also afraid that I was about to be handed a piece of information, a single fact or detail so far unrevealed, that would cause my whole trembling ethical position to crumble. I dreaded discovering that I had become cold-hearted; that a happy marriage, after all these years of fighting men, might have undermined my sympathy for my own sex, and weakened my moral imagination.

It was in this state that I picked my way, one May evening, through the maze of stud-walled, hideously papered corridors into which Melbourne University's Law School has been divided. I was fifteen minutes early for my appointment with Dr M——, a law lecturer, and her door was closed. On it were taped several news items and cartoons with a feminist slant, including a *Farrago* cutting of a statement by the Vice-Chancellor about 'extremists' who, he thought, were creating resistance to the feminist cause. I experienced a sharp stab of solidarity, remembering men who, over the early years of the women's movement, had given us the benefit of their advice on how best to conduct our 'cause'.

At exactly 6.20 p.m., the appointed time, a small slim woman with short dark hair arrived at the door with a key. She looked in her thirties, with a clear, bright face and steady eyes. She held her chin high, and gave off a toughish vibe: someone clever and determined, who had an agenda, as they say. Her hand, when she shook mine, was very narrow and hard.

Her room was large, with a high ceiling. It overlooked trees and could have been beautiful, but it was amazingly disordered. I sat in a chair and waited while she got her messages off the answering machine. She explained that she was writing a paper for a conference, 'about men who murder their wives out of jealousy or because they're leaving them – this in itself is considered sufficient provocation, so that a bloke like that can get three years while someone who does an armed robbery gets fifteen.'

She took me to University House, the academics' club on campus, and there I laid my cards on the table. She said she couldn't answer any questions about the Ormond case because she was 'too close to the complainants'. Thus, our conversation was general and, to my surprise, very enjoyable. Made wary by the anger of Christine G—, the Women's Officer, and the abuse of Barbara W— on the phone, I had not expected this. We disagreed on almost everything, but her manner was so clean and open, so good-humoured, that our disagreements were not darkened by offence given or taken. I outlined to her the sense I had got from several people that Colin Shepherd was a good-hearted naïf who had been thrown to the lions by the establishment he had aspired to be part of.

She considered this with apparent interest, and remarked, 'You seem to be de-gendering the story; whereas Cassandra Pybus in her book was re-gendering the Sydney Sparkes Orr case.'

'No,' I said, 'I don't want to de-gender it completely. I just wonder if sex wasn't only one strand in a much more complex story.'

'*I* think,' she said, 'there should be an absolute rule that there are no sexual relations between staff and students at a university.'

I stared at her in amazement. 'But how could this be enforced?'

'It can only be enforced by the student. If the student doesn't want to prosecute, there's no evidence.'

'How would it be found out, then?'

'The staff member's colleagues would know,' she said.

'But that would mean *dobbing*.'

'There should be a dobbing mechanism,' she said firmly.

'We should have the moral responsibility to call our colleagues on this behaviour.'

'But what if it's love?'

With the patient severity of a mother or a headmistress, she smiled and raised her eyebrows. 'If you fall in love – well, you just have to wait.'

'Or else you can leave the institution, I suppose,' I said, trying to follow the thought.

She shook her head sharply. '*She* can leave the university,' she said. 'I've got a gender analysis of this. Staff can't leave. There are no jobs. The law is about changing people's behaviour – and it *is* changing. We don't have wild drunken parties any more, with all the nineteen-year-old students. Students should enter the institution and find it to be the state of affairs, that staff-student relations are forbidden. At some US universities they already have this kind of set-up.'

'Isn't this a bit bloody Islamic?' I said. 'Do you think you have a chance of introducing it? Who'd be against it?'

'Men,' she said with a shrug. 'Civil libertarians.'

'Would dates be allowed?' I asked. 'Could you go to the movies, or have a coffee? What about holding hands? Where would the lines be drawn? And by whom?'

By this time we were both laughing; but she meant it. 'Holding hands would be . . .' She put out her hand palm down and wiggled it, meaning *a bit dodgy*.

Speechless, I sat looking at her. She looked back at me firmly, smiling, not budging an inch from her position.

'I'm interested,' she said, 'in working out what's sexual about sexual harassment. There's not enough recognition of the *power* academics have over students. At least we can empower students to realise that they are not in an equal power relationship.'

I didn't want to argue against *that*; but she pressed on to suggest that 'in heterosexual sex there's an eroticisation of domination'. Her tone here was almost clinically detached. I argued, rather surprising myself as I went along, that there *is* no such thing as an equal relationship, sexually or in any other way. Dozens, scores of examples from my own life flooded into my mind to support this thesis. I said I thought all relationships were power struggles – or that at the very least the power balance in every relationship is constantly shifting. 'You and me, for example,' I said. 'We haven't been together long enough to know, yet, which of us will be the stronger.'

She seemed a bit taken aback. Maybe as a lawyer she was suspicious of psychology; or maybe she was just shocked by how old-fashioned my feminism was – the sort she would presumably label 'libertarian' like Bettina Arndt's, whose name she had mentioned earlier in dismissive terms: 'She still has that *Forum* mentality, that more sex is good automatically. It's a very sexual-liberation model. Feminists have made inroads into our understanding of that.'

She spoke about the rape laws in Victoria, how in 1992 'fear of harm' was included as one of the admissible reasons for not consenting: 'Consent means free agreement. This requires men and women to *talk* about it. It makes things marginally less spontaneous, of course. Teenagers will be more stilted – bad luck. We need to move the discourse so sex is seen as a mutual engagement.'

I raised the question of women's passivity in disagreeable minor encounters with men, the paralysis of will, the sense of the terrible fragility of men's egos.

'Well, that brings us back,' she said, 'to what I was saying in my office, about men who murder their wives to stop them leaving, or because they've been having an affair.'

Again this point of helplessness: the instant raising of the stakes, so that further inquiry about the woman's role in a minor incident looks like treachery.

Outside it was dark. We walked back across the university grounds in silence. I asked her if she would concede that an affair with an older man could ever be 'a good thing – a *liberating* thing'. She pulled a sceptical face. I said, 'Back in the fifties, with Orr for example, the person in the street automatically assumed the girl was the baddy, the liar. Even women made that assumption. Now it's the opposite. The world's imagination is that the bloke must have been at fault.'

She shot a look at me. 'No! I don't agree at all!'

I said that this had been my impression, as I went about the town obsessively bringing up the topic with everyone I met.

'People in the *university*,' she said, 'didn't assume that the man was the bad egg.'

'Yes, but people in the university aren't like people in the outside world.'

She laughed. We shook hands and parted. On my way home I thought with relief that I would never have to be a student in the university Dr M— was envisioning. But I also felt exhilarated by our discussion. Maybe I *was* just a naïve old libertarian, while she was a well-trained lawyer, but I was impressed by the rare quality she had, the ability to separate her ideas from her ego, so she could radically disagree with you without having to hate you or deny you a voice.

~

Not for the first time a fantasy occurred to me: before people make pronouncements on what sexual behaviour society should tolerate, they ought to make the clearest possible statement of their own sexual experience, what they have learnt from it, and how it might colour their attitudes. 'I have a horror of penetration.' 'I am involved with someone who satisfies me sexually.' 'I would rather have a backrub than make love.' 'I'm only sexually attracted to other women.' 'I feel free only when I masturbate.' 'I have never had an orgasm and don't know what all the fuss is about.' 'I was molested as a child and still see men's sexuality as furtive and monstrous.' How would it change the way we talk about sex and power, if we had the self-awareness and the honesty to acknowledge psychological states as such, instead of passing them off as pure intellectual beliefs?

~

One night I dreamt that I was about to be shown over Ormond College. There were two women guides. One was a noisy, talkative, opinionated ideologue whom I disliked. The other was quiet, modest, retiring. I couldn't get a sense of what sort of person she was. Her manner was subdued, almost muffled, as if she didn't want to declare herself, or show her nature, yet.

~

I went to the Panorama in Brunswick Street to see a dreadful 1959 British movie called *Expresso Bongo*. One of its main characters is a pretty young blond called Maisie who works in a club as a stripper. Throughout the story she is constantly being approached by sleazy men, and has perfected a line in brush-offs which she delivers in tones varying from briskly casual to venomous. 'Seek elsewhere,' she snaps, without even looking up. Later, while she is having a drink with Cliff Richard (hardly any girl's idea of a protector), a drunk staggers up to their table and slurs, 'Whadya doing after the show, shweetie?' She fixes him with a glittering eye and enunciates with vicious clarity, 'Going to meet my boyfriend from the *Vice Squad*. Want to come?'

Yes, yes, it's only a movie, from a benighted era, and one is supposed to deplore her occupation and the fact that she is subjected to these advances – but how refreshing her bluntness was, her irritable wit, her stable sense of her self, of the precise whereabouts of her boundaries.

~

The senior lecturer in humanities, Dr Q—, who had thought his post-graduate tutor might be willing to give me the complainants'-eye view of Ormond, reported in a puzzled tone, 'When I asked her if she'd talk to you, she told me a little story about Colin Shepherd. She said that one evening, while the students were standing behind their chairs in the dining room waiting for the High Table to take their places, he went past her on his way in, and he tickled her.' Dr Q— made a two-handed gesture of grabbing someone round the waist from behind, affectionately, as one would to tease a child. 'And she said to me, "I'd never been so humiliated in my life – I felt like bursting into tears." I found this an odd reaction. And about you she said, "Yes, I've heard she's been *sniffing around* Ormond. You either believe those women or you don't. I do, and I'm not having anything to do with her." She said that as far as she's concerned, it's "a closed issue".'

Blocked again. Oh, they were so *wretched*.

Dr Q— had his own small story to tell. The year before, he had been warned by a female colleague that, according to graffiti in the women's toilets and carved into a desk in the Baillieu Library, he had 'abused his power'. The graffitist also urged students to 'provoke and report'. Since Dr Q—, a decent, open man, had always felt strongly about the issue of professional relations on campus, he was very exercised as to the meaning of this attack on his reputation.

'I racked my brains,' he said, 'for students I'd horribly antagonised. Finally I thought that maybe blokes like me, who make all the right noises – who claim to be capable of redemption – are the worst of the lot. At least with rednecks women know where they are, whereas blokes like me just sweeten the pill of the patriarchy. I was frightened, though. Frightened the rumour would get around that I was a sleaze-bag. For months, whenever I approached my office, I looked to see if there was any graffiti on the door.

'Humanities is where the action is, in terms of feminist theory. I had a very animated discussion with one of our tutors here about Colin Shepherd. She would have hung, drawn and quartered him on the *spot* because some women had made complaints. But in the same discussion she spoke admiringly about Madonna – said she was "carving out a sexual space for women". But if anyone *touched* her – look out!

'We ran an induction program for the post-graduate students who were going to do some tutoring. One session was on professional dealings with students. Several of the new tutors told me that I must never, ever talk to a student with my door closed; that if a student came to see me, I must insist on the door being open.'

'And do you?'

'I leave it up to the student,' he said. 'If *I* shut the door, it's a statement of my power. It may seem intimidating. Some of them come rocking in here and sit down with the door open behind them. But if the student shut the door and *I* opened it, it would be saying, "This is a fraught situation, a fraught relationship."

'These are very smart, bright, confident young women we're talking about here. But some of them said they didn't like the way blokes in their tutes looked at them. One of them told us that at the end of her class a male student came up to her and asked, "Is it all right for a student to ask a tutor out?" She was flummoxed by this. She said to us furiously, "This sort of thing must *not* be allowed to happen!" I said, "For God's sake, just make it plain that you don't *want* to!" I told her that eighty per cent of people in marriages and relationships meet in the workplace. How are people supposed to meet? I told them they would get infatuated with people they work with, people they teach – after all, they're only a few years older than some of their students. I said, "These things happen, and there are professional ways of dealing with it." They're so *fragile*! They have to learn to *deal* with it, instead of going'– he threw back his head and covered his face with his hands – 'Oh my *Gahd*!

'There's a woman connected to our department who's in her eighties. She's got no time for this stuff. She rounded on the young tutors. She said, "People like you think we're brains on stilts. You must realise that every tutorial is a dynamic event. Nothing will stop people from becoming infatuated."'

'What is this *about*?' I said. 'They arm themselves against wolves – that's right, it's good – but then some harmless bunny blunders into the headlights and they give him both barrels. It's inappropriately aimed. Is it referred anger, do you think? From the real outrages that you see in the paper every day?'

'I *hope* it's about real outrages,' said Dr Q—, without conviction. 'Rape, and silly bloody judges, and blokes that bash women.'

~

A woman in my French class, a Labor Party activist for all her adult life, told us in her careful, formal French that she had met the Prime Minister at a party in the electorate of Melbourne Ports. She said she had approached him, after he had spoken on various current issues including the Mabo decision, and asked him whether the government was seriously committed to resolving the terrible problem of white relations with Aboriginals. He replied with apparent sincerity that it was – and while saying this he put his hand on her forearm. She added that when she had described this small incident to people she knew, they had reacted variously. Several had gasped about the Prime Minister's hand on her arm: 'How condescending!' But more had said, 'How *sexist*!' When she told us this I felt a bomb of fury and disgust go off inside my head. *Sexist!* This has become insane.

Every day now I waited for the professor's daughter to answer my call and my letter. But from her direction streamed the silence that was becoming so familiar on the complainants' side of the story. In my heart I knew that the professor's daughter was someone whose voice I was fated never to hear.

~

By now I was becoming an obsessive listener on the topic of sexual harassment. As soon as I mentioned in casual conversation what I was trying to write, the woman I was with would give me a sharp look, pause, then pour out a story. One day, for example, I went to have lunch at the house of Nina D—, a friend who lectures in English, a clever, handsome young woman with a husband and two small children.

'When I was in my early twenties,' she told me, 'I went overseas to do post-graduate study. The university I went to was full of interesting radicals, and one particular lecturer was magnetic. I was reading stuff that put me through a fundamental re-appraisal of everything I'd been taught. My semi-Leavisite views were being torn asunder. It was terribly compelling. Every square inch of me wanted to be in this man's classes, and yet at the same time I didn't want to seem over-enthusiastic – I didn't want him to think I was *uncool*. I couldn't find a way to get the whole situation under control.

'He was very territorial with me, intellectually. When I'd talk enthusiastically about some lecture I'd heard by one of the other people I admired in the department, he'd say, "I don't *want* you to go to those lectures." He'd ridicule other people's opinions.

'I was impressed – but he was a *wolf*. He had a rapacious physicality. There was an incident in the car park – he was sexually insistent. I was always trying to keep him away and yet at the same time to keep him *charmed*.

'Halfway through the year, when I still thought he was magnificent, he said to me, "My wife and I are going away on holiday. We've got a house in the country and a dog that needs to be fed." I stayed in their house for ten days – it was lovely. But the night before they were supposed to return, he arrived back alone. That night he made me dinner, and at the end of the meal he attempted a seduction, which I fumbled. I said, "No! I don't want this!" I could feel him getting hard, I got panicky, it was all out of control. I ran out and got into my car and drove back to my share house near the university.

'When I got home, he rang. He was *cold*. He said, "You're right. What I did was unforgivable."

'And then he spent the rest of the year punishing me.

'He accused me of being a cock-teaser. He became very chilly towards me. I found it hard to arrange supervision sessions for my thesis. He seemed to care less and less about my work. Then the time came to give a seminar on the work I'd done, to the tutors and all the other graduate students – a roomful of twenty or thirty people. I started to read my paper. After the first sentence he broke in with a derisive comment. After every *sentence* he said something derisive. It was an orchestrated campaign to disallow me from finishing a thought.'

Her voice trembled and she stopped talking. I asked her what the feeling in the room had been.

'It was *electric*,' she said. 'No one said a word. No one said "What the fuck is going *on* here?" I had an almighty struggle not to burst into tears. I was thinking, "This is irreparable – this is *gone*."'

'I had quite a few friends in the department – tutors – who were feminists. I'd been trying to tell them what was going on. No one believes me when I tell them this: they thought it was *funny*. They laughed it off. They said, "Isn't that just like him. He's so *sexual*" – as if it was part of his cutting edge. Deal with him, deal with his dick.' Here she sounded puzzled, and uncertain. 'Maybe I told it to them ambivalently – or as a joke? I might have invited this response – anyway, they couldn't read my panic. I was so out of my depth. I didn't know what I was doing. I wanted my *mother*.' She laughed, but painfully. 'Anyway – this bloke subsequently fell from grace. It became clear that there had been case after case, before me and after me – a chain. I guess that sort of intellectual charisma always runs out. People started to say, "I always thought he was an arsehole." His colleagues began to loathe him.

'My question is, how does a girl like me, an extrovert, capable of handling herself in the world – how could I have failed myself in this instance? I was trying to be cool, but I was unable to get the right tone. I didn't want to lose him as my teacher. I didn't want to be cold-shouldered, rejected, intellectually put to one side.

'If I spoke to him about it now, he'd say "You were a coquette" – but the thing I remember most about myself was that I felt like an old-fashioned prig. In a way I did play at being flirtatious – I did play the passive, gasping girl – but now with distance I'm able to say, "Fuck that! I wasn't *asking for it.*" I wanted to be in a sparring, healthy intellectual relationship without its being seen as flirtatious.'

After lunch I had to go to a press screening of an Australian movie, *The Heartbreak Kid*, which was soon to be released; Nina decided to come with me. We took a cab downtown, bought some lipstick at DJs, and went to the cinema. The central relationship of the movie turned out, ironically, to be a love affair between a female high school teacher and one of her sixteen-year-old students. In the toilets afterwards we called out our opinions of the film to each other from our cubicles. She asked me whether I had liked the sex scenes. I said I had, a lot.

'Well,' she said, as we emerged and approached the basins and mirrors side by side, 'that touches on something I maybe should tell you. Which bears on what I'd told you about the problem with my supervisor, and maybe undermines my position.'

'What?'

'When I was first tutoring, up in Queensland, I slept with one of my students. Twice.'

I stared at her. We both laughed wildly. There was no one else in the toilets. We got out our new lipsticks and began to apply them.

'He wasn't cut out to be at university,' she said. 'He

hated my subject. There was a kind of joke around the place that he was so beautiful and sexy. I'd just broken up with a bloke who was very important in my life. There was a party at the end of term. And after the party we went home to my place together.'

Watching her in the mirror, I could not imagine their encounter being anything but joyful. 'I think you're both lucky,' I said.

'But don't you think it's immoral?' she burst out. 'I think the student's father in *Heartbreak Kid* was right when he accused the teacher of having betrayed his trust. You *are* in loco parentis, with students. Don't you think so?'

'In high schools, yes – there's a point there,' I said. 'But not in universities. And there are *major* differences – it's not as if you manipulated him, or attacked him, or distorted his intellectual life or tried to humiliate him publicly, like your supervisor did to you. It was a mutual attraction, wasn't it?'

'Yes – but how can I still complain about what my supervisor did, when I've done something like *that*?'

A whole novel lies shadowed in her story. The erotic will always dance between people who teach and learn, and our attempts to manage its shocking charge are often flat-footed, literal, destructive, rigid with fear and the need to control. For good or ill, Eros is always two steps ahead of us, exploding the constraints of dogma, turning back on us our carefully worked out *positions* and *lines*, showing us that the world is richer and scarier and more fluid and many-fold than we dare to think.

~

In May the *Sunday Age* ran two big front-page stories with sexual themes. The first was a piece about a serial rapist who was terrorising the Ascot Vale area, where, as it happened, my daughter lived. This man's latest victim was a woman in her eighties. The second piece, illustrated by a large colour photo, concerned women police who dressed as prostitutes and enticed motorists in St Kilda to pull over to the kerb and make sexual propositions; at a given signal, the policewoman's backups emerged from hiding and arrested the driver.

I didn't know how to read the juxtaposition of these stories. It could have been a simple desire to sell papers, though the *Sunday Age* probably thinks of itself as a quality paper. Perhaps it was an attempt at balance: we can't catch the rapist, but we can come down hard on these gutter-crawling pervs in St Kilda: we can be seen to be doing something. Fear blurs the skid in reasoning here, from *rapist* to *would-be customer*: and it *is* a skid, whatever your position on prostitution. The spectacle of policewomen offering themselves as decoys in a campaign against prostitution is cold comfort to women who have excellent reason to fear random sexual attack.

Next day an *Age* journalist reported that the frightened women of Flemington and Ascot Vale 'want better street lighting. They want more police car patrols of the area. They want posters and notices about the attacks and the suspected man in shop windows and on billboards. They want community outrage to have an effect. The worrying fallout of these attacks,' the journalist went on, 'is that women then feel it is their responsibility to defend themselves against rape.' She quoted a spokeswoman for the Centre Against Sexual Assault: 'But it's not a woman's responsibility to defend herself from rape; the responsibility for the prevention of sexual assault belongs to men and the community.'

I thought for a long time about this statement. How can it be argued? I believe that rape is an outrageous crime, that it should be taken much more seriously by police and courts than it often is, that it should be very severely punished. When in 1994 the Ascot Vale rapist got thirty-four years I was glad, glad, glad. Ethically, yes, it *is* men's responsibility not to rape women; but I don't understand how 'the community' can prevent sexual assault while yet allowing women the freedoms we demand: the right to live alone, to go about the streets as we wish, to drive cars, to drink in bars and dance in clubs, to work for our living alongside men, to travel on public transport, to walk or run on beaches and in forests. How can there be such a thing as *safety*? Even totalitarianism can't make women safe. There can't be freedom without responsibility. It *is* a woman's responsibility to protect herself against sexual assault. A free woman must accept that in the world there is risk – that risk is part of her freedom.

~

I read Cassandra Pybus's re-examination of the Sydney Sparkes Orr scandal, a story which was still being whispered about in 1961 when I got to Melbourne University. In those days Suzanne Kemp, the student who claimed to have been sexually involved with Professor Orr, was almost universally reviled; the misogynist assumptions and behaviour of men of every stripe in the Australian academic world of the fifties, as laid bare by Pybus, are breathtaking. I instinctively understand a woman like Suzanne Kemp. I am closer to her in age, background and experience than to an Elizabeth Rosen or a Nicole Stewart. These days young women are assumed to have more sexual knowledge and experience than we did as students. I remembered, as I read Pybus's retelling, going to my first party in Trinity College in 1961, herded over from Janet Clarke Hall in a batch of trembling freshers. The party was held in the room of a second-year student who is now a successful barrister. He offered me a beer. I primly replied, 'I don't drink anything alcoholic.' The high, nervous voice in which I made this statement still rings in my ears, making me blush. Is there still such a thing as 'innocence'? As Nina D—, the woman whose post-graduate supervisor preyed on her, said to me, 'I wanted to be *sophisticated*.' Frank Moorhouse says somewhere in one of his books, 'Why are the innocent ashamed of their innocence?' It's as if there were a way of becoming experienced other than through experience itself.

~

One of the people I interviewed for this book lived in Trinity; for the first time in almost thirty years I walked into that college's Clarke building. Naturally it seemed much smaller and less imposing than I had remembered. Its brutal hollowness had been muffled by carpets. The landing windows were of stained glass: this I had forgotten, or were they new? As I passed them, I glanced out on the northerly side and saw that the building where I first slept with a man – a *boy*, for God's sake – was no longer there. It was absolutely gone, and its site was now occupied by a car park. I also recalled, as I climbed the stairs, a night a year or so later when I slept, against all rules and customs, in the narrow bed of my second boyfriend, who was also my tutor. We had been drinking at the football and after; he had passed out. When I needed to go to the lavatory in the middle of the night, I put on his dressing gown and scampered along the hall to the bleak, freezing bathroom.

On my way back to bed, I saw a student coming out of a room; I turned and dashed back to the toilets and shut myself into a cubicle. I heard the student come into the outer section of the bathroom and stand there non-plussed: he must have seen me. I waited in silence behind my door. His footsteps receded again into the hall. I tiptoed out of my cubicle and peeped down the corridor towards my boyfriend's door. *The student was tapping on it.* Oh God – I was trapped. I ran back in and locked myself in again. My feet were bare and freezing on the concrete floor.

I heard distant male voices murmuring. After a while there was silence. I crept out and back down the empty hall to my boyfriend's room. 'Where the hell have you been?' he said as he let me in. He told me that a student had knocked on his door and said, 'Mr X— – I think there's a *woman* in the bathroom.' The concept of the nerd did not exist at the time, but may be applied retrospectively.

Postscript: When my tutor got a famous scholarship and went to Oxford, he broke my heart, of course. I sobbed in cafés and hotel bars, bored my friends half to death, and thought myself tragically bereft. I cannot in all honesty claim to have been 'liberated' from anything in particular by my relationship with this man. I hated his subject and was bad at it, failed it twice and did not care. He made me laugh, that's the main thing I remember. I often felt he was privately laughing at *me*, from the eminence of his twenty-four years. This made me watchful and defensive. But I learnt from him two things: firstly, to start an essay without bullshit preamble, and secondly, that betrayal is part of life. I would have learnt the betrayal lesson anyway – perhaps I knew it already; but it probably helped to have it made clear to me early on. Anyway, until I wrote this account of being trapped in the Trinity dunnies it had never occurred to me to call what happened between me and my tutor 'sexual harassment' or 'abuse of power'. It was a relatively minor episode, seen in retrospect, and it ended wretchedly, but I value it as part of my store of experience – part of what I am and how I have learnt to understand the world.

When Colin Shepherd abandoned his struggle for re-instatement and did at last resign, the *Age* of 25 May 1993 handled it discreetly, giving the matter eight brief paragraphs on page two, headed *Chief quits 'untenable' Ormond job*. (This discretion may have been prompted by a complaint Dr Shepherd had lodged with the Australian Press Council; the APC later adjudicated in Shepherd's favour, criticising the *Age* for 'a serious omission in terms of balance' and calling the concluding part of the article in question 'unfair'. The fact that Dr Shepherd had received a substantial order for costs against the police should have been reported, according to the APC.) The *Australian*, however, ran the news on the front page with a big photo and the headline *Sex-row Master quits*. The photo showed Dr Shepherd peering out from behind a half-open screen door, its frame made dramatic by the spiky shadows of leaves. He was dressed in a collar and tie under a striped cotton football sweater. It was an image chosen by an editor with a ruthless news sense: it made Shepherd look furtive, wary, hunted – as if the photographer had shot him against his will, in the act of slamming the door. An old neighbour remarked to me, 'What an evil face.'

Shocked by her reading of the photo, I scanned it again. To me he looked stricken, desperately unhappy, nervous – but *evil*?

Later that day I had a call from the journalist who had written the accompanying piece for the *Australian*. She told me that when she and the photographer had visited Dr Shepherd at his house he had welcomed them inside and spoken courteously to them. The photographer had taken plenty of good shots inside the house. He and the journalist had been upset by the paper's distorting choice of graphic.

The journalist asked me some questions for a piece she now wanted to do about the fact that I was trying to write this book. I spoke very carefully, outlining my doubts and trying to express my sadness and frustration at being denied access to the students' version of the affair. Next day this piece was run. Late in the day I spoke to the journalist on the phone. She told me that the complainants' solicitor had rung her. The girls had read the article. They were 'very shocked and upset'.

At that moment something inside me snapped. I wanted to find Elizabeth Rosen and Nicole Stewart and *shake them till their teeth rattled*. I saw my polite attempts to contact them and their supporters as unbearably naïve, my hopes for a response from people like Professor J—'s daughter as pathetic. The daily papers were awash with endless outrages against women, as if victimhood were the sum of our experience. Feminists were redefining themselves in these terms, dragging themselves on bleeding stumps to the high moral ground of survival. To try to draw ethical distinctions, to point out gradations of offence, to suggest that women were in possession of untapped power, was now an act of treachery. I realised that I was wasting my time. I was just about ready to throw in the towel.

~

But the day after the press reported Colin Shepherd's resignation, I received an unexpected phone call. It was Professor J—. I recognised at once his prim voice, a strangely audible way he had of breathing through his nose between sentences.

'Helen Garner? Um – what is your *address*. I need to send you a *letter*.'

My stomach dropped. I gave him my address and spelt out the street name. Quickly and without further niceties he thanked me and said goodbye. I hung up. What on earth was this anxious feeling? It was exactly the physical sensation one gets when the principal says, 'Report to my office in fifteen minutes': the childish Ur-fear of *getting into trouble*, of being punished for some nameless, unknown misdemeanour. At fifty, one locates this dread in one's psyche and tries to deal with it there; but it struck me that this story, for the students, must have been studded with such moments, as they drove themselves to confront professors, barristers, magistrates, judges – the whole apparatus of power in its panoply, under the banner embroidered with the small but resonant word *Master*. The women's motives might baffle and infuriate, but there was something impressive in their determination.

I thought that after all I would not give up. Not quite yet.

And besides, I was eager to know what Professor J—'s letter would say. I began to rush home from work each afternoon, looking for the mail.

~

A friend gave a small dinner party for her birthday. Four women were present, two Australians, one German, one French, some of us previously strangers to each other; but we talked till long after midnight. We agreed that over the past few years, as we approached fifty, we had ceased to feel 'at the mercy of men'. The Frenchwoman, the youngest of us at forty-seven, said, 'But I still have red flashes of rage.' She told us that in her mother's provincial café, when she worked there in her very early teens, men used to put their hands up her dress, and her sister's; she used to hate this, but did nothing about it until one day a man did it once too often. She spun round and hit him so hard that she broke his glasses. We all applauded, laughing. She went on, 'But my mother was annoyed with me. She said he was a really good customer.' We uttered cries of protest. She added, 'Once a priest who was confessing me put his hand on my thigh. I never said anything to anyone about it – but I never went back to church, either. I consider that a much greater betrayal than the other.'

Then the other Australian said, 'My girlfriend and I were both raped, as teenagers.' She slid this into the conversation so casually that we were all taken aback. The German woman, who had known the speaker well for many years, leaned forward and cried out, '*Raped*? You never told me this!' The Australian shrugged, looking completely matter-of-fact. She wasn't trying to shock us, or even to up the conversational stakes. We stared at her, waiting for the story.

She said nothing.

I said, 'Was it somebody you knew, or was it a stranger?'

'It was a doctor.'

Appalled, we sat in silence. She didn't go on, only said,

'I was eighteen. I never told anyone about it – not till many years later, when a friend and I were talking once, and she told me *she'd* been raped, at fifteen, and had also never spoken about it afterwards.'

Later, as I was driving her home, I asked her about it again. She said, 'Actually, he was an abortionist. A well-known sleaze. I went to him to find out if I was pregnant.'

We looked at each other, and away. There was another long silence.

'Do *you* understand,' I said, 'why women and girls go passive, when men attack them or approach them sexually?'

She shrugged. Perhaps it was too late in the evening for a couple of middle-aged feminists to open that particular can of worms: the complexities of what our lives as women had shown us about power, sex and assault.

I woke up the next morning sad and anxious, aware of the immense *weight* of men on women, the ubiquity of their attentions, the exhaustion of our resistance. In such a mood it seemed to me an illusion that women could learn to deal with this pressure briskly, forcefully, with humour and grace. I thought about the complainants, Elizabeth and Nicole, and I felt deeply sorry for them.

~

I'm sick of hearing the blokes' side, the institution's version. Why won't you talk to me? I'm sitting here waiting to be convinced, but no one will come out of the bunker and argue it. I can write the book without your version – I can imagine it, for God's sake! – aren't I a woman? – but it's so important. If you have a case, why won't you put it to me?

Months later I found this plaintive pencil draft of a letter to the young women's supporters shoved into my files at this point. I never copied it out or sent it.

~

It wasn't till twenty-four hours after the conversation with the women at dinner and in the car on the way home that I recalled one crucial fact in the Australian's story of the doctor who had raped her. 'The worst part,' she had told us at the table, 'was that I *paid* him.'

It astonished me that I had forgotten this detail; but the fact of my having forgotten it underscored its importance. And I noticed that when I did remember it I was filled with a sense of immediate, deep and total empathy: an effortless understanding of an act which one would have considered, with one's rational mind, to be grotesque. And it reminded me of a disagreeable (if much more trivial) experience of my own, which until this moment I had never written down or tried to analyse, though I had often thought about it with bewilderment.

In the early eighties I used to do aerobics at a gym on Johnston Street in Fitzroy. Every couple of weeks I would treat myself to a massage. The masseur, a man of about my age, had his table set up in a tall, narrow, windowless space between the gym's reception area and the women's change rooms. It had two doors and was dimly lit by a high fluorescent strip. One thing I liked about this masseur was that he didn't feel the need to entertain you with a stream of chatter. He worked in silence. This meant that his massage produced a condition of extreme relaxation, almost a waking dream-state. He was very skilled, and I'd been to him at least half a dozen times.

One day I booked myself in. 'Haven't seen *you* for a while,' he said as I undressed and climbed on to the table. I explained that I'd been broke and busy, and he began to work. The only interruption was his request, half an hour later, for me to turn on to my back. He worked from my feet upwards. When he had finished with my right arm and was laying it down, he kissed the back of my hand.

I was thunderstruck. I couldn't believe it had happened. I thought I must have dreamt it. I lay there as if everything were normal, but I was tense and alert, though I still hadn't opened my eyes. He continued to massage me: left arm, abdomen, chest, shoulders, in the ordinary asexual way. Then he moved to the top of the table, stood behind me, and took my head in both hands, as he always did, to massage my neck; but I felt his face come down over mine, and he kissed me gently on the mouth.

I didn't move. I lay there, flat on my back and stark naked except for the towel he had spread over me as he worked. I kept my eyes tightly shut. I was unable to compute what he had done. I was more than anything else *embarrassed*. He finished the massage without further incident. At the end of it I opened my eyes and got off the table. I could hardly meet his eye. My face felt stiff with awkwardness. Something needed to be said, but my mind was blank. While I was pulling on my track suit he said, with a calm smile, 'Don't let it be so long, next time, between visits.' I recall thinking in amazement, surely you don't imagine you'll ever see me again? But still I said nothing and made no sign.

I said goodbye – I think I even smiled – and scuttled out of the room. I got my bag out of the locker, fronted up to the reception desk, *and I paid.*

What else might I have done?

I might have said to the woman manager, 'I'm not paying for this massage. The guy came on to me without provocation.' Would she have believed me? Had other clients complained? Would she even have thought it mattered? No – what *she* thought about it was not the point. This was between me and the masseur.

I might have opened my eyes and said to him, 'Don't do that. I don't like it. Just do the massage.' But he had broken the professional contract between masseur and client, the unspoken agreement that makes it possible for a woman to take off all her clothes in a closed room in front of a stranger without its having a sexual meaning: it would hardly have been possible for the massage to continue, once his act had been acknowledged.

So I behaved like a child. *I kept my eyes shut.* That is, I declined to take any responsibility in the situation. When I left the room I was still maintaining the pretence that nothing untoward had happened. And I never went back.

And this is where my masseur's kiss loops back and touches Nicole Stewart and Colin Shepherd on the dance floor, in her version of the story which the judge 'did not disbelieve' but which could not be proved. What woman would not feel a shot of rage at the QC's question to Nicole Stewart: 'Why didn't you slap 'im?'

We all know why.

Because as Nicole's friend said angrily in court, all we want to do when a man makes a sleazy, cloddish pass is 'to be polite and get away'.

What did these students – clever, beautiful young women in their twenties who drive, vote, drink, dance, wear sophisticated clothes and have free sex lives – what did they do when one of their friends ran out of a party upset and told them that the Master had groped her? Their spontaneous collective action was to make it look *to him* as if nothing untoward had happened – to cover up the unpleasantness, to smooth things over. Instead of making clear to him their true feelings about what their friend had reported, they offered themselves to him (even if 'for less than a minute') as dancing partners, as decoys. They believed they were protecting Nicole from him; but in fact everything they did was directed at protecting *him* from knowing that he had offended her.

Is it retrospective shame of our passivity under pressure that brings on the desire for revenge? Is *revenge* the right word, or should it be *retribution*, the term used by Christine G—, the fierce Women's Officer, with its atavistic clang of righteousness? Again and again come these sharp flashes of empathy with the girls; but something in me, every time, slams on the brakes to prevent the final, unbearable smash. I invent and discard a dozen fantasies of less destructive responses to such an incident. I remember a tutor from another college who told me about having to drag one of his colleagues out of a party where he had been 'monstering' the women students: 'We took him outside and shook him and said, "Listen, mate – *they don't want to fuck you!*"' I see myself marching into some man's office and saying, 'I know what you tried on my daughter. This time I'm prepared to let it pass. But I'm warning you – if anything like this ever happens again, you can expect big trouble.'

One of the sweetest men I ever knew, my first father-in-law, used to say, 'Even a dog gets two bites, before they put him down.'

~

'A bloke came up to me in a pub,' said a 24-year-old student, 'and said, "Can I buy you a drink? You've got a beautiful *bod*." I opened my mouth to say, "Why don't you fuck off?" – and then I suddenly thought, he's just a poor bastard. So I said, "That wasn't a very good thing to say". He took it fine. He turned out to be a boring nerd, of course, but his friend was quite nice. I think I'll try that sort of response from now on. What's the point of making them feel humiliated? They never learn anything, that way.'

Once more I tried to get in touch with Nicole Stewart and Elizabeth Rosen. I wrote to each of them, and sent the letters in care of their solicitor.

> I'm aware of a rumour currently being circulated, to the effect that what I am putting together is a 'pro-Shepherd version' of the events; I'd like you to know that this is untrue. My aim is to write a truthful, calm and balanced account of what happened, to set it in a wide social context, and to try to understand what it means. If you remain unwilling to speak to me, I will go ahead with the project anyway, but it seems a pity that the first book on this important subject should not include your two voices. I know you have both suffered a great deal and I respect this. If you would consent to speak to me, I would be very glad.

I sent letters as well to as many of the girls' supporters in the university as I could identify, by guesswork, association or rumour. Deep silence ensued. As a group they maintained facelessness and voicelessness – in my direction, anyway. People I knew, both women and men, would stagger back from academic dinner parties, book launches, literary festivals, meetings, and report to me in amazed detail their encounters with feminist women who claimed to be among the girls' supporters, or to have friends who were. All these women knew *exactly* what sort of book I was writing, and they wanted nothing to do with it, or with me. 'But if you spoke to Helen,' my friends would argue, 'she wouldn't be *able* to write that sort of book. By *not* speaking to her, you're making it impossible for her to write anything else.' All argument, my friends said, was vain. 'There's no *possible* way they'll speak to you,' they told me. 'They say that what you're doing is "part of the nineties onslaught against feminism". They say old-guard feminists like you "don't understand the issues in their current form". They say you're "incapable of being a journalist". They say you've been "constantly harassing" them.' Against this frustration I worked to maintain what used to be called 'an open mind'. But I was in a state of bewilderment and scorn. What sort of feminists are these? What kind of thought-police, of saboteurs?

Or don't they believe in the strength of their own argument? Will they only speak to people who already agree with them? We used to truck out and present our views to the Werribee Young *Farmers'* Association, for God's sake. But since post-modernists tossed the idea of truth out the window, Milton's great challenge has lost its poetic ring. 'Let *warrantable assertion* and falsehood grapple'? I hardly think so.

~

I went to lunch with Dr K—, the retired academic who had rebuked the post-graduate tutors for thinking of intellectuals as 'brains on stilts'. In her eighties, she was a slim woman with beautiful bones and bright eyes, dressed in a chic black suit and a white blouse. She told me, as we walked across the campus, that she was Freudian-trained in London. 'I'm interested,' she said, 'in what makes minds tick.'

Her movements, at the table, were slow and careful. Her manner, though, was almost seductive: she was a practised charmer. At the table, while we talked and ate, she would look sharply straight into my eyes, but would sweeten her directness by tilting her head to one side and suddenly giving a wide, closed-mouth smile that turned her eyes to slits. Maybe this was the manner a clever women of her generation had had to devise, in order to live out her intellect without its frightening people and making men hostile; always I could sense her mind at work behind the smiling, time-marked face.

She mentioned that at one point in her career she had been the only woman, and the only non-professor, on her University Academic Board. 'I was a not unattractive woman at the time,' she said with a sly smile, 'and I capitalised on it. A lot of women, in the world of men, spoil their chances by *over-talking*.' She, I noticed, had firm control over her natural old woman's tendency to ramble: whenever her discourse strayed from the point she would draw it back briskly, saying, 'But we weren't talking about *that*.' Occasionally she would trail off and sit thinking privately for a moment.

'It's the time we live in,' she said, when I outlined the Ormond story to her, and mentioned the current climate in sexual harassment thinking. 'We've got a cock-eyed view of human relations. We think of relationships in terms of people who fuck – not in terms of their emotional content.

'There are other forms of power than the directly sexual. There can be mother-son relationships within a department, or father-son, or father-daughter. These aren't contra-indicated. Some universities have a no-husband-and-wife rule, but none has a no-father-and-son rule.'

She spoke with a sort of terse, worldly tolerance of 'poor old mutts' of men who find themselves charged with sexual harassment in colleges and universities. True to her Freudian training she dug under the literal in search of telling imagery. 'Maybe what happens in some of these cases,' she said, 'is a symbol for the sexual act itself. Maybe the old dears aren't after sex at all but acceptance. It's naïve to assume they're only after erotic gratification – they mightn't even know what erotic gratification *means*.

'At my age, in retrospect, I'm not concerned at all about who grabbed who. I'm only concerned about what I understood about people, and what they understood about me. People are basically afraid of being *moved*. There's not much generosity, much giving. It's "Don't touch me – you might make me come out of my shell". People now are so defensive. What's so precious about the sanctity of one's "space"? My goodness – haven't they ever slept with someone to *comfort* them?'

As we were leaving the restaurant, Dr K— fumbled at the counter, trying without her reading glasses to identify our bill among several lined up there. A man of my age was standing beside us. She looked up at him with her flirt's smile and head-tilt, and said in a high, sweet, self-mocking voice, 'I can't find *meeee*!' The man laughed, and quickly located the right bill for her. She was old enough to be his mother, but the rules of the playful encounter came spontaneously to both of them.

I admired her performance, and her knowing spirit. Walking home, I thought of her symbolic angle on sexual harassment, her suggestion that what a man longed for might be not sex but acceptance; and I remembered the photo I had been shown on my last visit to Ormond: the solitary man in the football sweater, trudging along on the muddy grass, gazing towards the oblivious backs of the students watching the match. At a pedestrian crossing on Princes Street I waited for the lights next to a young woman on a mountain bike. She was a big-shouldered, powerfully built girl with short hair; under her helmet her face was pugnacious and grim. She had glued a sticker along the frame of her bike. It read, *'Exactly which part of* N O *don't you understand?'*

~

'This obsession with sexual harassment,' said an old friend, a woman in her fifties, 'is just a diversion. It's not the main thrust of the women's movement. A man in Shepherd's position must not do the things he was accused of.'

'It's terrible to me,' I said, disconcerted, 'to see the effects of this on his life – on his family.'

'Oh,' she said, 'I don't believe he *deserved* what's happened to him. He may be "innocent" – but he's paying for many, many other men who have *not* been caught. It's the irony of things, that sometimes the innocent or nearly-innocent pay for what the guilty have done.'

Yes, and you can't make an omelette without breaking eggs: what a cruel and ethically rotten argument. Another feminist I know went very quiet when I tried to tell her of my discomfort with the Ormond story. She related a painful experience of sexual interference from her child-hood, and went on to say that 'in any period of change, innocent or half-innocent people are going to get caught in the crunch.' She said this as if it were to be accepted without protest or even regret. If I'd had my wits about me I might have quoted Janet Radcliffe Richards' tough and useful book *The Sceptical Feminist*: 'If justice does not matter in transitions, it does not matter at all.'

Instead I got upset, and stammered an objection: 'How can this be right? How can this be ethical, that punish-ment is skewed like this – so that the wrong person carries the can?' She looked at me with a kind of accusing surprise. There was an awkwardness between us when we parted. Once again I looked hard-hearted, on the wrong team, a turncoat, lacking political passion and solidarity.

But twenty years in what used to be called the counter-culture have taught me to be wary of the word *solidarity*. I've seen hesitant people bludgeoned by an appeal to solidarity. Solidarity can be used to mock genuine doubt, to blur a fatal skid in reasoning. Run the flag up the pole and see who salutes. Whenever I feel in myself the warm emotional rush of righteousness, of belonging, that accompanies the word *solidarity*, I try to remember to stop and wait till the rush subsides, so I can have a harder look at what has provoked it.

That winter of 1993 I spent days in the Ormond library, reading the minutes of the college council, the General Committee of the Students' Club, and the Equal Opportunity Committee that Colin Shepherd had set up to advise him on policy where male/female relations in the college were concerned.

The EO body's records were presented in a disconcertingly tiny typeface. A chill came off that tininess, that rigour and thoroughness. The committee's final document, its recommendations to council, opened with an attention-getting stroke: a demand that the Aboriginal tribe on whose land Ormond College stands should be recognised, acknowledged and commemorated. While this might appear farfetched to some, it brought to me a sharp memory of the fact that when there was first a push, at Melbourne University, to establish a women's college, certain men took out mining rights on the proposed site, to prevent this from happening.

The minutes of the General Committee of the Students' Club, over the period of Colin Shepherd's troubles, were by comparison cobbled together in haste. Members were identified by nicknames. There was no sense at all of the high-level drama that was unfolding in the college, only a concern for fun and more fun: parties, sport, grog, 'bumblebees' (Ormond striped sweaters), computers – and a demand, if you please, for a dispenser of free condoms. It was a ratbaggy, tedious, occasionally charming stream of jollity.

The minutes of the council proper, each meeting of which was 'constituted by prayer', were formal and sparse, with little meat on their bones. I was inclined to skim. But after a while I began to develop a feel for significances, a sense that there was a sub-text to be read, even if I could perceive it only dimly: when certain persons left the room and returned to it; corrections to the previous meeting's minutes, for example when one of the women's supporters had objected to a mention of her having accepted 'on behalf of the complainants' Melbourne University's offer of its conciliation services.

I noticed how, once Colin Shepherd came on board, there was an injection of warmth and energy into the dry proceedings. His contributions, in reports and speeches attached to the minutes, were humming with enthusiasm – but they were also sprinkled with droppings of the word *tradition*. I wondered whether the use of the word might be considered *pas comme il faut*, a little gauche, by dyed-in-the-wool Ormond men. At these points Dr Shepherd seemed very much the newcomer, not yet versed in the institution's codes, even teaching his grandmother, so to speak, to suck eggs.

Soon came the proliferation of sub-committees whose reports, because of the press leaks, were too confidential to be included in the minutes; and then the painful realisation, as I read Dr Shepherd's bouncing report of his first full year in the job, that as he delivered it he must have had not even an inkling of what was passing through the heads of some of the people who sat with him round the table, listening.

On 25 November 1993, exactly six months after his resignation, a 'minute of appreciation' of Colin Shepherd was added to the council records, seven or eight hundred words detailing his career in Education, his honours (including the Order of Australia 1989), and his achievements during his brief Mastership. The tribute describes him as 'a man of engaging enthusiasms', and speaks of his 'vigour of mind and person'. Its final paragraphs run thus:

> In March 1992, allegations of sexual harassment against the Master were made public and over the succeeding months and despite his being cleared of charges brought against him in the courts, his position grew to be untenable and in September he stood down as Master. In May 1993, the council accepted Dr Shepherd's resignation with regret. The council places on record its appreciation of the service rendered to the college by Colin Shepherd as Master and its awareness of the deep pain suffered by him and his family in the circumstances of his leaving.

~

Still I received no letter from Professor J——. I hoped against hope that he would keep his nerve. Everyone I asked about him spoke well of him: 'Oh, he's a straight-shooter. An honourable and decent man. A good Christian. Someone who tries to be as kind as he can.' Yes, but his dilemma would try a philosopher or a saint. By innocently telling

me the story from the complainants' point of view he had
got offside with their faction: he must be under pressure
to recant.

~

I went to buy some meat. My butcher, behind his counter
in Carlton, hears everything and looks at the world with a
sceptical eye. He asked me what I was working on, and I
told him. While he wrapped up my chicken he told me
what gossip he'd heard about it. He glanced up at me
constantly, waiting for my opinion. After I had left three
or four pauses unfilled, he raised his eyebrows. I said, 'I'm
working hard at not saying anything.' 'Oh!' he said with a
laugh, 'I wasn't trying to draw you out – just making conversation.' I said, 'There's a big push on, these days, against
sexual harassment.' 'Yes,' said the butcher, straightening
up and handing me my parcel, 'but where does *my* world
fit in? I'm a Catholic. I went to Catholic schools. A priest
tried it on. I said no. Years later I was flattered! To have
been *liked*!'

Liked? Oh, we are all so lonely. Under these stories lie
great chasms of self-doubt, uncertainty and fear.

~

How had Colin Shepherd got the job in the first place?
One morning in early winter I drove out to Canterbury
to put this and other questions to Mr Douglas R—, a
retired member of the college council. The street he lived
in was sloping and handsome, its wet pavements thickly
strewn with red leaves, but his house was a plain 1960s
cream-brick dwelling, set high on a neatly trimmed garden
block. As I hurried past the wooden hutch for milk bottles

(a rolled-up cheque stuck out of the neck of a sparklingly clean empty) and mounted the concrete path to the door, I picked up a whiff of a delicious plant-smell. It reminded me of something, but I had no time to pause and identify it. Mr R— greeted me at the door, without offering to shake hands. He was an old man of slight build, with white hair parted and combed down, and was dressed in neat, firm-fitting clothes, Henry Bucks style, with the old brown brogues buffed to a glossy sheen that are a badge of his class, his profession and his generation. He ushered me into his study. Seated, he looked more commanding. He examined me with the steady, appraising gaze that psychologists and lawyers use: *I'm listening. Why are you here?* I heard myself begin to chatter nervously, but suddenly remembering the remark of the old woman who had taken me to lunch, about women who 'miss their chance' through over-talking, I bit off my sentence, and he launched into his, exactly as if my babbling had not happened. I felt both squashed and relieved.

'It ought to be obvious to everyone,' he said briskly, 'except some of the people behind this story, that the final result is *utterly* out of proportion to the case. In fact, when the first charge appeared in the papers my eldest daughter lined up *her* daughters and said to them, "If anything like this ever happens to you, and you don't deal with it yourselves in a better way than this, I'll *disown* you." '

Ouch! I was glad that in my fantasies of something unpleasant happening to *my* daughter I had at least gone in to bat for her.

At the time when Colin Shepherd was appointed, he said, there had been about seventy applications. On the reduced list there had been three or four women, most of whom had got on the list 'because of their backgrounds'.

'What do you mean by backgrounds?' I asked.

He looked down at his hands, which were reddened and puffy, with fragile-looking skin. 'I'm old,' he said, after a long pause, 'and it's three years ago. They had quite reasonable *academic* backgrounds. The Master should be able to take a reasonable place in the university academic community. There were some fascinating applications,' he continued, slipping with relief on to less fraught territory. 'One chap had been in the New Guinea highlands for many years, imparting education. He wrote that "a more relaxed form of life" would suit him.' He laughed. 'He was discarded early on – but I would have liked to fly him down. *He* would have had some interesting stories to tell!

'When you work doing these things, when you're accustomed to reading CVs, you come to realise that some people have something they're escaping from. But Colin Shepherd presented himself as someone who felt that the Master of Ormond was just that thing he'd love to be – and he did love being it, too. Not just because of the prestige, but because of the whole complexity of circumstances surrounding it – contacts with people, responsibilities, variations of the managerial skills the Master is called on to display – academic, administrative, personal.'

Mr R— spoke at considerable length and with pointed emphasis about the way Dr Shepherd's appointment had been received 'by the community. He was favourably known by an enormous number of people. I had letters from people I'd never heard of, saying Ormond was to be congratulated on having got him. A man I regarded as a total stranger stopped me in William Street to say what a good thing it was. It was very gratifying. When you're selecting people for these higher appointments, at the end you're keeping your fingers crossed – so if someone comes at you making reassuring noises, you're pleased.'

I asked him whether he thought people had been out to get Shepherd.

'Not before the allegations,' he said, 'but plenty were, after.'

'Who do you mean?'

He shrugged. 'Oh, no names no pack drill.'

A cuckoo popped out of a clock and called the hour. 'It's eleven o'clock,' said Mr R—, standing up. 'I'll put the kettle on.' He soon returned carrying a tray of plunger coffee and a jar of home-made biscuits. He took a biscuit for himself and put the jar on the small table beside me. I ate one. It was excellent, the absolutely perfect biscuit. I remarked on this, and took another, then perhaps another. Ten minutes later, without breaking off what he was saying, he got up from his chair, walked over to my table and replaced the lid on the biscuit jar. He was halfway back to his seat when he suddenly stopped, turned towards me, and said, 'I didn't do that to keep *you* out of there!' We both laughed. But I thought, yes you did, sir – you were putting the lid back on what you know: I won't get any more out of *you*. Unnerved by his gesture, I asked him, 'How did this thing blow up so dreadfully and get so out of hand?'

'If I were you,' he said, 'I'd explore the reasons for the delay in bringing the complaints to the Master himself. They were not conveyed to him. There was a possibility, you know, that Monash University would give him his job back. But there were anonymous phone calls, threatening that trouble would follow him there if he was taken back.'

'What sort of troubles?'

'Continuing demonstrations, I suppose. You can get up a demonstration about anything, in a university.'

'Do you have any idea who the callers might have been?'

He looked at me sharply, with a sly smile. 'I'd examine the *dramatis personae*,' he said, 'and see if there's one that fits. There might be two. Possibly Colin Shepherd has suffered one of those almost tragic injustices that can wreck various aspects of a man's life – a *person's* life, these days. And those who brought it about – let's say – don't deserve much praise.'

Mr R— saw me to my car. On our way to the front door, he stopped in the sunny hallway and showed me a watercolour on the wall, a picture by Harold Herbert of a flat desert town in North Africa: rows of white houses, a strip of blue sea on the horizon, and in the upper corner a plane streaking away. 'This is my prize possession, at the moment,' he said. He thought it was a town he had been in during the war. He mentioned Rommel. 'We got the Italians out of it,' he said.

'It's a beautiful picture,' I said.

'It's more than beautiful,' said Mr R— severely. 'It's *accurate*. It's almost all white, and yet the white contains different colours as well.'

I resisted an impulse to dawdle, to ask, 'Do you often think of the war, now you're old? Does it seem very close to you? Was it the best time of your life?' It occurred to me later that his desire to mention the war to me was similar to my urge to tell Christine G—, the stern young

Women's Officer, that I had worked in the abortion law reform movement: '*We* helped to change the abortion laws.' It was a way of saying, 'I may look weak to you now, but once I was young and strong.'

Passing through the garden on the way down to the gate, I caught the plant-smell again and recognised it: a certain moss that grew round the roots of an oak tree in my grandparents' garden. It's a scent that always evokes in me the memory of being young and about to visit someone old with whom I shared a tender affection. All the way home I cursed this trick of nature, and my slowness at dragging it up to consciousness. I realised too that Mr R— had told me hardly anything. Like the old lawyer he was, he had skilfully blocked my amateurish questions – and not only that: some instinct had caused him to play the father to me, in exactly the way that would bring out in me the prodigal daughter: respectful, unchallenging, emptied of girlish rebellion. Disarmed by the smell of the moss, I had walked right into it. It took me days to think clearly about the interview.

As one who had keenly supported Shepherd for the position of Master, Mr R— might have had egg on his face had he not swerved robustly away from the question of sexual ethics and steered straight towards the conspiracy camp in whose tents (once comfortable, now rather draughty) he would presumably have encountered many a colleague of his generation. One powerful and widely respected university woman had spoken to me tartly about Mr R—'s domineering style on committees: 'If he doesn't want to,' she said, 'he just doesn't *see* you.' An even more highly placed man described him as 'tough as hell. When he fixes you with those pale eyes, he's a force to be reckoned with.' It still alarms me that I rather liked him – that we *got on*. When I got home and mentioned the Harold Herbert painting to my husband, who knows a lot about art, he said, 'Harold *Herbert*? Oh, he's a *very* conservative painter. Very, *very* conservative.'

~

Not long after this, I spoke to one of the women who had been on the reduced list for the Ormond job when Colin Shepherd was appointed. 'Although I got to interview stage,' she said, 'the majority of the council wouldn't have appointed me. One of the older men in particular was antipathetic to me – he kept suggesting I wasn't academically senior enough. This is a classic way of getting rid of a woman – specially one with children – you say she's under-qualified *for her age*, even though the man she's up against is less qualified than she is, and the status gap between her academic discipline and his is *huge*. There was one woman on the committee; I could feel she was carefully containing her enthusiasm. But I felt, I could never *work* here. It seemed a bastion of privilege, and the men were *horrible* – except for one, who had a more encouraging manner. I lost interest. This counts in your favour, in an interview. It means you don't care, and so you say things more forcefully. I could hear in my own voice that I was disengaging from the whole idea of it. I was sitting there thinking, God – what a *crew*. Imagine monthly meetings and weekly meals with *this* lot.'

Writing a review for a newspaper of Hazel Rowley's biography of Christina Stead, I went back to several of Stead's novels and was swept away once again by her vitality – her embrace of life, her respect for and delight in the power of sex.

> In a moment more the door opened and Léon appeared, fully dressed and very fresh. Behind him was a dazzling young woman, a Ukraine blonde, with a long plump face, a complexion of radishes in cream, hair in page curls. Her eyes, large as imperial amethysts, roved in an indolent stare of proud imbecility. For a full minute after the sudden splendour of her entrance, Aristide Raccamond found himself bathed in her glare . . . She advanced with studied insulting vanity. Her manners were perfect, that is, she flouted the Raccamonds outrageously, stirred the eels in their souls, while she went through the polite ritual minutely and coaxingly.

Comparing the opening scene of *House of All Nations*, so funny, free and grand, with the mingy, whining, cringeing terror of sex as manifested in the Ormond story, I felt as if someone had flung open the window of a dark and stuffy room. Take away the imbecility, and the 'Ukraine blonde' of that passage could be a description of someone like Elizabeth Rosen – what eels have been stirred in whose souls by that brilliant and wild young creature? – and yet according to the Equal Opportunity statement, Elizabeth Rosen thinks of herself as a 'worthless sex object' when her beauty and her erotic self-presentation arouse desire in men. Something here has gone terribly wrong.

~

In the kitchen at a birthday party a woman I have known for years, who has a long history of involvement with the left, leaned towards me out of her chair, hot-faced and angry, to press her argument against men who harass women. Her large, flexible hands gestured as she spoke; when she disagreed most vehemently, the right one made a vertical wall between us, its palm towards me, six inches in front of my face. Above and behind this barrier, her handsome face shone with zeal. I tried to listen well and to be calm: *I did not want to fight.* I said, 'Yes, violence against women is terrible – it's wrong – but I don't think violence is what we're talking about, here.'

She said hotly, 'What about waking up, the way *I* did once, and finding a man bending over me, naked, wanting me to suck his cock?'

'Yes – but would you agree that something appalling like that is of a different degree of seriousness from a man dancing with a girl, say, and letting his hand touch her breast?'

'*Letting?* You said *letting*.'

'You're right. That's the wrong word. Let's say, *putting*.

Putting is what's been alleged. *Putting* his hand on her breast?'

'Okay,' she said. 'There *are* degrees. But there's an underlying *assumption*, in both cases – in *all* these cases – which is *the same.*'

'A man isn't tried on his assumptions, though. A man is tried on what he *does.*'

We sat simmering. An old friend of both of us, a man who helped us to bring up our children in the big households of the seventies, was sitting with us. He listened calmly, making no comment. The bottom of my stomach started to weaken again. *Have I lost something? Abandoned something? Have I joined the other side?* Then she spoke again, but in a different tone of voice, vaguer, more thoughtful, shifting her gaze to a distant point in the room, over our shoulders. 'And I *was* in *his* house,' she said. 'It's not as if I was in my own bed at home and he broke in.'

The stories older women tell about unpleasant sexual experiences: first the blunt statement, the rage; then the pause; then the qualifying remark, the introduction of the ambiguity.

~

Dr V—, one of the women's angry supporters, appeared to me in a dream. I came across her in a house, on a broad stair landing. She raised her head from a book she was examining, and greeted me. She looked slight, pretty, clear-eyed, open-faced and warmly friendly. I knelt down beside her and we examined the book together, with our heads side by side, like sisters. Cut to a car. She took the wheel. Suddenly the road dropped steeply in front of us and became deeply rutted and slippery with mud. She eased the car down the terrible road, her small, nicely shod foot on the brake. I was tense and apprehensive, but not scared; she seemed competent, but *my* intelligence and nerve were feeding into what she was doing.

~

Still I had no letter from the straight-shooting Professor J—. Could he hold out? Was he too losing sleep?

~

I phoned a prominent feminist writer in another state, with whom I was slightly acquainted, to ask her advice.

'Yes,' she said, 'I've heard you're writing the pro-Shepherd version.'

'Who told you that?'

She named Rose H—, one of the women's supporters who had not answered my letter. I took a breath, and outlined my actual approach to the matter. Her manner warmed slightly.

'Sexual harassment has gone off the rails,' she said. 'Not because the charges are trumped up, but because it's *damaging* people.'

In a later conversation she told me about an appointments committee for an academic job. 'The obviously best person was a woman. They wanted to appoint her, but she had a small child and needed flexible hours. "Oh no – we can't do *that*." So the job went to the next person, a man, who was less qualified. This is the terrible thing,' she went on. 'What we hoped and worked for was that a thing like that didn't need to happen. We wanted flexibility – but all the energy that might have led to changes in this area has been turned around and focused on this narrow, punitive business of sexual harassment.'

In the course of researching this book I have heard many such stories from frustrated university women. 'There was a chair,' one of them told me, 'and a short list of three people – an American woman, utterly brilliant and appropriate; a colourless man; and an awkward, unclubbable but original man. Guess which one they chose? The colourless man. You can see why women get so mad – then a bloke in a powerful job slips up, and even if it's a minor matter that could have been resolved by other means, the women have got up such a head of steam that they think, oh, this is *too much* – we have to make an example of him or they'll go on getting away with it for *ever*.' Another woman academic, near retiring age and warmly respected by men and women alike, said to me, 'Sometimes I think that nothing will change without people who are prepared to go *way* beyond what is considered reasonable. Maybe extreme behaviour is the only way to shift things.'

The interstate feminist writer told me that she had spoken to Nicole Stewart and Elizabeth Rosen months earlier. I asked her whether they had had to agree to maintain confidentiality as a condition of their settlement with the college.

'No, they haven't,' she said. 'I advised them not to speak, though. I told them that the best thing Suzanne Kemp could have done, when Cassandra Pybus was rewriting the Sydney Sparkes Orr case, was to remain silent. They're prepared to talk to someone, now – but not you. In fact, they're going to talk to *Vogue*.'

Vogue! I gnashed my teeth so hard I saw stars.

When I got home from work I found that the *Vogue* journalist had been trying to contact me. I rang her number and got an answering machine which told me she had *gone to Bali*. I left the politest-sounding message I was capable of.

~

The *Age* reported the case of a young woman whose step-father had sexually molested her for years, when she was between the ages of ten and sixteen. When this was discovered, she was made a ward of the state, and kept *in Winlaton girls' home* for eighteen months. Much later he was charged, given a very light sentence, and released after serving only seven and a half months of it. Soon after his release the girl, now a young woman, was driving her car when she saw him on the road. She aimed the car at him and ran him down. He was quite seriously injured, and she was now up on a charge. She named herself in the press, and her photo was published on the front page. I read all this with hatred and rage, and with a sense of exhilaration at what she had done. Some acts of revenge are cleansing strokes. Fate offered his body to her and she seized the chance. Most of all I respected her bravery in having identified herself publicly.

One bitterly cold morning in June 1993 I rode my bike downtown and arrived with streaming eyes and nose, and fingers barely capable of holding a pen, for an eight-thirty appointment with Mr Donald E—, one of the Ormond council members who had been authorised to force the affair to a conclusion, in that they had negotiated financial settlements between the girls and the college, and between the college and Dr Shepherd.

'Some council members,' he told me, 'have had a very emotional reaction to the thing, which has made them a bit of a menace. They thought we should have done much more to keep the Master there – that we should have fought the girls to the death. Some of these people wanted a full council inquiry – they really wanted to get amongst it.

'To us, it was more important to get Ormond back on an even keel. The truth was at the bottom of a well. Though it stuck in everyone's gizzard to settle the thing, we *had* to settle it. Because of the leaks we couldn't conduct such sensitive negotiations with the knowledge of the full council. So a small group was voted in; and laboriously, in order to avoid an EO hearing, five of us negotiated a settlement.'

The terms of this settlement, he said, were confidential, and he would not give the details. Later, other inquiries I made suggested that money was paid to the girls, a substantial amount. Part of the settlement, too, was that the students were to take their records away.

'There are four or five people who stayed in touch with Colin Shepherd,' said the council member, 'and encouraged him to believe that someone on a white horse was going to come along and save him. We're not very popular. We've received letters from even the Archbishop of Canterbury protesting his innocence.'

I stared at him. 'The Archbishop of *Canterbury*?'

He grinned, and made an airy gesture with one hand. 'Oh, that's just an ambit claim.' He got up and showed me an extract from a letter that had been lying on his desk: a sad, angry letter, awkwardly typed, its errors corrected in trembly biro. It contended that Colin Shepherd had been denied natural justice; that if the courts had cleared him he ought not to have lost his job.

'People have been rounded up,' Mr E— continued, 'to write to us and say, "Hey – you're murdering this fellow." But there was nothing anyone could do. He was too badly winged.'

There was a brief silence in the sparsely furnished, glass-walled office. There might have been a sigh; but if there was, it probably came from me.

'What behaviour,' I said, 'do *you* think is required of a Master?'

'The Master has to be like Caesar's wife.'

'What does that mean?'

'Above reproach.'

It took me a moment to absorb the strange conjunction

of such a feminine image with the word *Master*. So Caesar, in this analogy, must be the college, or its council.

'Colin Shepherd's main weakness as Master,' Mr E— was saying, 'was that he was too close to the troops. He wanted to pull on a football jumper and run around on the riverbank. Perhaps he'd spent too much time at Somers Camp.'

'What *is* Somers Camp, exactly?'

He looked surprised. 'It was originated by Lord Somers, the one-time Governor of Victoria, so that boys from privileged and under-privileged backgrounds could be together during the summer. And well-meaning adults joined in all the fun.

'The Master's got to *manage* the college. You need – though I don't much like using the word – charisma. You give Ormond its tone. And you have to make sure it's a happy place for people to work and study in. Since we advertised the position, we've had a hundred and ten letters from people wanting further particulars. We'll probably get fifty more.'

'I guess Colin Shepherd must be pretty crooked on you all,' I said.

'He doesn't seem to be, actually. We wrote to him and thanked him for having been gentlemanly in his conduct throughout. We tried to help him with other jobs. When you think of all the wickedness in the world, what he's alleged to have done doesn't rank all that high. Nicky Stewart seemed to me a very sophisticated young lady. Why didn't she just knee him in the balls?'

~

I came away from this interview, as I did from many with the men who run the college and exert power in the wider community, feeling obscurely unsettled. I had to acknowledge that I was putty in the hands of these old stagers, with their racy turns of phrase, their imagery drawn from sports and war, their confident bandying of biblical and Shakespearean references. On a day when you don't feel personally at its mercy, the discourse of power is seductive. It is worldly. It enlists and flatters you. It can afford to relax and be genial, to charm and entertain and take risks and crack jokes. The clincher is its humour: Eros, 'the spark that ignites and connects', flashes into the room on the charge of laughter, disarms with a sudden vision of the absurdity of the whole ghastly mess, and leaves women looking grim and dull and wowserish and self-righteous, struggling against men in the name of boring old justice.

But feminism too is a conduit for Eros. Women's struggle for fairness is a breathing force, always adapting and changing. It is not the exclusive property of a priggish, literal-minded vengeance squad that gets Eros in its sights, gives him both barrels, and marches away in its Blundstones, leaving the gods' messenger sprawled in the mud with his wings all bloody and torn.

~

What always impresses me about Monash, coming as I do from the older University of Melbourne with its elms and dank courtyards and buildings made of stone, is how Australian it looks. In winter the wind charges across its open spaces, fiercely jostling the eucalypts and making their leaves sparkle in the cold sun. From out there, Ormond might seem a century away – a distant, forbidding, old-world fantasy.

'Monash made the decision not to have colleges,' one of its senior administrators told me. 'We've got halls of residence. It's much cheaper. You get a better mix of people, you get Asians – and it breaks down all that funny cultural stuff.'

Twenty-one years full-time at Monash had not prepared Colin Shepherd for the 'funny cultural stuff' he encountered at Ormond. When he applied for the Mastership, after sixteen years as senior lecturer in Education, he must have had his head pressed hard against his personal academic ceiling. The Ormond job was a way forward for him – a big jump. 'And after any big jump,' the administrator said, 'a whole new set of enemies emerges.'

For someone with little experience of institutions, it is startling to be offered a glimpse behind the scenes – to see how a man who has come a public cropper may be hauled off-stage by a bunch of impatient colleagues in the wings, dusted off, and discreetly slid back into the performance – only in the back row of the chorus for a while, perhaps, but still working, still drawing a salary. This might have worked for Colin Shepherd. At the time of his resignation from Ormond he still had warm support from erstwhile colleagues in Education at Monash. 'I had verbal assurances,' Dr Shepherd told me, 'from high up in Monash adminstration and from the Education faculty, that everything was fixed – but no letter ever came.' University positions have to be advertised. To get round this there is the notion of the paid consultant. While subtle negotiations were afoot, however, a senior administrator at Monash received some surprising phone calls.

'I believe,' I said to him, 'that you were strong-armed.'

'Strong-armed!' He dropped his head into his hands and turned his face away. For a moment I thought he had been offended by my choice of word; then he looked back at me with a crooked, ironic smile which I took to mean that 'strong-armed' was putting it lightly. 'I got at least three phone calls,' he said, 'towards Christmas 1992. Three women, anonymous, with youngish voices, got through to me. *I* became the bloody issue! They said, "Don't think this is going to stop here." They were . . . abusive. I slammed down the phone on one of them. They were out to get this man, and anyone who sheltered him was equally guilty.'

Meanwhile, there was a change of regime in the Education faculty. During this transition, support for Dr Shepherd lost impetus. Senior administrators of the university were reluctant to issue orders 'from the mountain'. Matters were not helped by Dr Shepherd's reluctance to be satisfied with whatever crumbs could be thrown to him. Another senior man at Monash told me that the position in Education had been 'fixed – there was a room for him, he had all his pencils and his paperclips organised – and then hints were dropped about an associate professorship.'

Strings were pulled by very powerful men, but something in Shepherd's demeanour, I was told, caused them to lose patience. He was too fussy. He had scruples about the reactionary politics of at least one business group that offered him a quiet berth. He was not prepared to eat the required amount of crow. Soon these men were no longer returning the calls of Dr Shepherd's champions. His behaviour, which seems so unreasonable and capricious, so lacking in the willingness to cut his losses and accept rehabilitation with bowed head, is explicable only if one keeps reminding oneself that Dr Shepherd has an unshakeable belief in his innocence.

~

On my way home from Monash that winter day, I drove past a certain house on a corner, and was overcome by a strange memory. In the early seventies I delivered to that house a silent and trembling woman from New Zealand who had flown across the Tasman for an abortion. I was just one member of a feminist organisation formed to help change the abortion laws and to work meanwhile at arranging safe terminations for women who were in trouble, who couldn't wait for the slow, grinding process of legal change. This woman was Maori, too shy to speak, completely out of her depth in a foreign city. I delivered her to the surgery and picked her up again afterwards. I took her to the shared house I lived in. My friends and our children sat with her at the kitchen table while I made her a cup of tea. She drank it in silence. We didn't even know how to talk to each other. She sat in our kitchen with her arms folded over her belly. Soon I drove her to the city, to the Queen Mary Club where accommodation had been arranged for her. Another member of the organisation must have taken over from me there; I have no further memory of her visit. Since then I must have driven past that abortionist's house scores of times, without ever noticing it. But driving home from Monash last winter, speeding along that ugly, endless road, I saw the house, and the memory of the woman's dark, frightened face rushed back to me for the first time in more than twenty years.

T he airwaves seemed to be humming with talk about sexual harassment. Whenever I turned on the radio, somebody was earnestly arguing it this way or that. One day I watched Donohue while I ate my sandwich. Sabino Gutierrez, a Hispanic with sculpted hair, told in a heavy accent and trembling voice of having been harassed for years by his female supervisor. Once she came 'to his condominium' and put it on him so heavy that they 'had sex'. He was 'terrified of losing his job if he said no'; he was 'very proud of his job'. A hostile white man in the studio audience asked him what present he had brought his boss on his return from a holiday. Sabino replied, 'A pair of pillow – pillow –' (glancing for help at his female lawyer) 'pillow covers'; the audience burst into scornful laughter. The rub was that a jury of twelve people – whose forewoman, a calm, articulate black woman in her thirties, was also, incredibly, on the show – had awarded Sabino damages of one million dollars for the loss of his job. People in the audience, smirking and grinning with hostility, asked him, 'Why didn't you leave the job?' 'Why did it take you so long to report her?' A young black woman asked, 'Why didn't you leave the very day she touched you on the genitals? *I* wouldn't have stayed.' While he stammered out his reply, she kept on ironically smiling and shaking her head.

His feminist lawyer, a tough motor-mouth in shoulder pads who got in a quick plug for having acted for the girl who claimed she was raped by the boxer Mike Tyson, made the point: 'Why should the *victim* leave the work-place? It should be the wrong-doer who has to leave' – and got a smattering – but only a smattering – of applause. Everyone's ethics seemed to have been turned upside down by the fact that the harasser had been a woman.

Next day I rushed to watch part two of the story. Sabino's ex-boss now appeared, the man who had had to fork out the damages after the court found the supervisor guilty. This unsympathetic personage, an overweight white man with a grey, stiff-looking ponytail, who sat with his legs splayed and seemed often about to explode with rage, had dealt with Sabino's complaints about the supervisor by sacking Sabino. By aggressive questioning, he got Sabino to admit on camera that he had only an elementary school education. 'Fourth-grade,' said Sabino, hanging his head; then, as his ex-boss trumpeted on about having replaced him *with a graduate in electrical engineering*, Sabino added faintly, almost in a whisper, 'But I work hard.'

At this I felt a stab of America-pain, class-pain, race-pain; and I saw once again the endless complexity of these stories, how the sex part is only one thread in a great matted *carpet* of struggle.

I also thought that one reason for the popularity and addictive nature of talk shows, specially the rehashes of trials, is that people in their hearts no longer believe that courts provide justice. These televised bunfights are a grotesque parody of a fantasy I repeatedly had when I covered the child-murderer's trial – a fantasy that there might exist some other forum, outside the harsh rules of evidence which excise context; some better, broader, freer, less rulebound *gathering of the tribe*; a forum in which everything might be said, everybody listened to: where bursts of laughter and shouts of rage might not be outlawed: where if people agreed to take turns everyone might at last, at last be *heard*.

~

One morning towards the end of writing this book, I had to call Mr Donald E— to check two factual matters. The first required a simple yes/no answer, which he gave. The second was more complex, concerning motive. Perhaps I spoke too fast, or failed to make myself clear; anyway, Mr E— misunderstood my question and launched on an explanation of the wrong thing. 'I've already told you this,' he added, between sentences. Although his tone was only faintly irritated, I became flustered. I tried to interrupt, to redirect his attention to what I needed to know, but because I was nervous I began to gabble. He paused for a second; then he rolled right over me. I subsided into silence. Incredibly, though I was invisible to him on the end of a phone line, I even went on taking pointless notes. I felt intensely foolish, like a child who has been squashed by a teacher. I felt *ashamed*. Stupidest of all, I didn't even have the aplomb, once he had finished his laborious and unnecessary reiteration, to correct his misunderstanding. I actually *thanked* him and said goodbye. Then I sat here at my desk like an idiot, flushed with astonished fury. I am fifty-one years old, and still at the slightest obstacle I regress into this ridiculous passivity. Why didn't I persevere? Was it because I would have had to make *him* look wrong-footed? Was I, like the girls at the Smoko, doing everything I could to spare his ego?

In New York last year I heard a well-known woman journalist give a talk about a recent trip to Eastern Europe. The applause had hardly died away before her host at the event, a male academic whose special field was European politics, aggressively challenged her on a factual point. She produced from memory a more recent statistic than the one he had used to contest her argument, and courteously laid it down – but as she did this, she blushed. *She said*, '*Sorry.*' 'Male power', 'patriarchal insensitivity' – yes, all this, with impatience and bad manners thrown in – but also *our* hesitancy, *our* feebleness of will, *our* lack of simple nerve. What *is* this fear women have of our own power – of just calmly taking hold of it, calmly putting it to use? Is there something in it for us, that a man's ego should have to be spared a minor dent? A woman remarked to me about a man who had pestered her with his attentions at work: 'He was a delicate plant. Older than me and with much higher status. I wasn't scared of him. I felt I could cope better with being a victim than he could have with being rejected.' An older woman told me about a fine and respected teacher she had had at university in the sixties, a man who at parties, after a few drinks, would hug his women students, rub himself against them, try to touch and kiss them. 'We would never have *complained* about him,' she said. 'We liked him – we were fond of him. And we felt *sorry* for him.' Whose *is* the power, in situations like these? There is a path here that might be followed, a line of fruitful questioning: but puritan feminists prefer to ignore it. They are offended by the suggestion that a woman might learn to handle a trivial sexual approach by herself, without needing to run to Big Daddy and even wreck a man's life, because it unsettles their unstated but crucial belief: that men's sexuality is a monstrous, uncontrollable force, while women are trembling creatures innocent of desire, under siege even in a room full of companions, forever about to be made to *feel uncomfortable*. I don't understand my own sporadic collapses into passivity. Perhaps I never will. But this analysis of power is of no use to me at all. In fact, in its disingenuousness it weakens me, and makes me ashamed to call myself a feminist.

I tried, on and off over a period of months, to contact several other young women students from Ormond whose names had been mentioned to me as companions of the two complainants on the night of the Smoko. I got nowhere. Doors were slammed by people unwilling to act as intermediaries. I was about to give up when I discovered, by chance, that the mother of one of them had been a friend of mine at school. I tracked her by a wandering route, back through my family and across old bridges to hers, and found her at last, by phone, at the place where she worked.

As soon as I heard her voice I remembered something I had always admired and envied about her: a way she had, while staying comfortably near the top of every class, of driving our women teachers out of their minds. Under pressure she was imperturbable; she just went on smiling a strangely enraging smile. 'It's easy,' she told me once, at sixteen. 'When they start to tick me off I sit here and imagine what they'd look like with no clothes on.' The smile was still in her voice, but also, now, when I stated my name and business, a certain steely quality. Her daughter, she thought, *wouldn't* like to talk to me about it.

It had been a disturbing experience to young people *without positions*. She, like the other girls, was disturbed that a book was being written. They felt it would crystallise them in some way. They had been uncertain, and they were still uncertain. Her daughter had resisted being called to give evidence.

'This might be a nasty question,' she said, 'but if *your* daughter had been involved in something like this, how would *you* feel if someone was writing a book about it? Would you want her to . . .'

There was a pause. I said, 'I hope I've brought up my daughter to believe in open discourse.'

Another pause. Then she said she would put it to her daughter, and get back to me. Several days later she called me. No, her daughter didn't want to speak to me. 'It's water under the bridge, as far as she's concerned.' She had taken my point, that everyone should at least be able to have the choice of speaking if they wanted to: she would try to contact the two other girls. If I hadn't heard from them by the end of the month, I should take it that they did not want to speak to me.

This was a low point for me, when we hung up. I thought my courage was used up. They would never ring, I knew; and of course they never did. But that day I phoned my daughter and said to her, 'I've been taking your name in vain.' I repeated to her my schoolmate's question and my answer. I asked her if she would have agreed to be interviewed, in such a situation. There was a short silence. I stood there holding the phone: my knees were trembling. Then she said, in her dry, thoughtful voice, 'It would depend on who was writing the book, of course. I can tell you one thing, though. I might have reported it to *someone* – but I would never have gone to the cops.'

~

And then, at last, Professor J—'s letter came.

It was typed very high on the page, and signed in a cramped, nervous-looking hand. He pulled the plug on the interview. He asked me to destroy my notes.

I asked a magazine editor I sometimes worked for whether I was obliged to do this.

'Of course not,' he said. 'They're yours. Some journalists would say that once a person's spoken to you, knowing it's for publication, you're legally in the clear to quote them, even if they ask you not to. It's a moral decision for you, now.'

So I continued to refine the art of not sending abusive letters. I wrote them – oh, I wrote them! I wrote furious insults on a bedraggled scrap; and then I tore it up and stamped it into the bin with my boot; and I took a fresh sheet of paper and rolled it into the typewriter and started again, more politely, more calmly, more falsely:

> Dear Professor J—,
>   I was very sad to receive your letter asking me to destroy the notes from our interview and to refrain from mentioning your name or quoting anything you said; but I acknowledge that this is your wish, and will respect it.

Early one Saturday morning not long after this, I went with a friend to the Victoria Market. As we were entering the meat section, a tall, stooped man hurried out past us. It was Professor J—. I don't recall now whether our eyes met. At the time I thought they did. I stopped short and looked back, but he was walking very fast, and didn't turn around. If I'd been alone I might have run after him – to say what? I don't know. Just to stand in front of him and see what *he* said. The one that got away.

~

In the August 1993 issue of *Vogue Australia* appeared a feature article on sexual harassment, by the journalist who had gone to Bali. I rushed to read it, hoping to hear at last the voices of Elizabeth Rosen and Nicole Stewart, their reflections in retrospect on the story, their characters; but once more I was disappointed. The journalist gave an account of the case which was warmly sympathetic to the complainants, set it in a sort of context, and spoke of the stress and health problems the women had experienced since the court hearings. But only one of the women had actually spoken to the journalist, and her remarks were strangely remote and formal. 'I don't regret making the complaint,' she said, 'because I think it was important for me, the college and the university. I had a lot of support from female staff, which was crucial, but the reaction of some male teachers was that they wouldn't see me without having the door open. Academics, particularly those who are part of the college's administration, are in a position of trust and responsibility, people to whom a student would go for advice about problems of an emotional, financial or professional nature . . .' She stated that it was not only the attitudes at universities but within the legal system which needed to change. 'We were asked questions in court,' she said, 'about what we were wearing at the time of the incident. I do not think that should have been relevant.' She added that she would welcome guidelines on staff-student sexual relations, 'but only if the university is prepared to implement them and act upon them.'

When the *Vogue* journalist returned from Bali, she phoned me. Her contact with the complainants, it turned out, had consisted of a telephone conversation with Nicole Stewart.

'How did she strike you,' I asked, 'as a person?'

'Very forceful,' said the journalist. 'She held an inflexible, politically correct line – as you do, when you're in your twenties. At that age you don't see greys. She must be feeling invincible. I asked her about you and your book – one of their supporters had faxed me your letter to Colin Shepherd. She said she wouldn't speak to you – not even if you'd changed your mind.'

I had a sudden sense of Nicole Stewart's having whizzed by me, very close – a scorched sensation. Who was this very angry, very forceful comet? All my thoughts, all my interviews and papers, suddenly felt hollow and savourless.

The winter of 1993 was over by the time I made my last visit to Ormond. I arrived early and hung about on a side doorstep of the huge main building, looking out over a lawn studded with native trees. A eucalypt stood against a pale blue sky in which, very high, a big black bird was cruising. It circled magisterially, with never a flap. Someone inside the building, way above my head, was softly playing a piano. Everything in the garden was 'so cool, so calm, so bright' that I began to be able to imagine how people – adults – might want to live there; how disgruntled women might be bothered making it into 'a contested site'. I remembered a student from Melbourne University describing to me how, while she waited one evening for an Ormond friend to emerge from choir practice, she had leaned over the balustrade into the courtyard as dark fell: 'Lights were coming on, I could hear voices talking quietly in the rooms that gave on to the quadrangle, and the choir was singing faintly, far away inside the building – and I thought to myself, my God, this is an *incredible* place!' I was beginning, reluctantly, to think the same thing, that lunchtime in very early spring, when the peace was shattered by a blast of heavy metal from upstairs, followed by a girl's playful shriek and the thunder of running feet. I stepped down into the garden just as the outside doors of the dining room opened and students poured out in twos and threes, on a tide of the unmistakable smell of institution food, the odour that no amount of scrubbing and swabbing can ever erase from a building, or from the memory of someone who has spent an unhappy year at a boarding school. What people will cling to, so as not to have to grow up, learn to cook, plan a household budget, manage their own lives! What people will bear, in exchange for having three meals a day put in front of them on a table!

When Simon T—, the Acting Master, arrived and took me to his pleasant apartment in one of the college buildings, I asked him his opinion of co-education in colleges. He replied warmly that he was '*strongly* pro. Ormond always got the best men,' he stated with jolting bluntness, 'and now, since co-ed, it gets the best women. There *are* winners and losers in this world.'

I digested this, remembering what a female head of one of the smaller Melbourne University colleges had said to me about co-ed: 'It's the God's police thing again. The presence of girls is supposed to address the disciplinary problems of the boys.' She had added an anecdote about an old churchman from another state who, at a conference, had expressed disappointment that, since his college had gone co-ed, the boys' behaviour had not improved at all – and worse, there had been no reduction in the food bills: 'I thought women would be cheaper,' he said. 'I thought they'd *eat* less.' The female head had shouted with laughter at this memory.

'Isn't there a theory,' I said to the Acting Master, 'that

co-ed is good for your son, but less good for your daughter?'

'Of course,' he said, 'we've got a hundred miles to go yet, before we get people to live together in a civilised way. But there's a trade-off. Though the female students tend to adopt male traditions, the blokes become less aggressive.' I asked him if he thought that the feminist group in Ormond which had organised against Colin Shepherd might have formed in opposition to this blokish element in the college. He cut across me in a flash. 'We've always had feminists in Ormond. We've always tended to attract strong-minded, independent women.' He spoke briefly about the fallout from the Shepherd affair, mentioning how expensive it had been for the college to settle the matter, and also its disturbing effects on general morale and on certain of the minor or background figures, of whom some had left the college, and others had not had their contracts renewed. 'But the student turnover will soon get it behind us,' he went on briskly. 'Elizabeth Rosen's younger sister was in college, but she moved out halfway through this year. All things considered, she preferred to live outside the college.'

The Acting Master went on to tell me that some council members had recently proposed changing the title of the head of the college to *Provost*, from the latin *praepositus*, placed in charge. 'They thought this would be a good time to change it, now that the name *Master* had been dragged through the mud.' Every level of the college community, he said, had been 'consulted in open forum – but it fell flat. No one was interested. They saw it as part of "that business". They genuinely don't care. They probably like the tradition, despite the gender.

'The appointment of the new Master,' he said, ushering me to the door, 'will be a cleansing moment.'

So soon! I thought, as I walked away across the magnificent gardens. The water will close over Colin Shepherd's head – or over his disappearing feet, as in Auden's poem: '. . . how everything turns away/Quite leisurely from the disaster . . . /. . . And the expensive delicate ship/. . . Had somewhere to get to, and sailed calmly on.'

The appointment of the new Master was announced in the press in November 1993. The professor of government and politics at Murdoch University in Western Australia would take up the post early in 1994.

Much later I heard, from someone who was working at Ormond on the summer day in March 1994 when the students were moving into the college, that the new Master looked around the vast entrance hall with its human-dwarfing scale and echoing polished floors, and said, 'It's so bare in here. Couldn't we bring a bit of those beautiful gardens inside? Even just a little jar of flowers on this wooden table?'

~

Meanwhile, having abandoned hope of a response from either of the two complainants or any of their supporters, I packed up my notes and papers and went to New York. I had been working there for several months, in that climate of intellectual openness which is so astonishing to an Australian, when I received one morning, long after I had forgotten her name or even the fact of having written to her, a reply from one of the Ormond women's supporters, a woman I had never met. It was scribbled in a looping hand, dead centre of a quarto sheet. 'Dear Ms Garner,' it said. 'Regarding your request of August 12th. I am not willing to talk to you now or in the future.' Over land and sea it had come fleeting in its neat striped envelope, and scudded on to my desk: one last forlorn brandishing of the feminist fist, enclosed in its tight circle of self-righteousness.

~

Why *did* Elizabeth Rosen and Nicole Stewart report Colin Shepherd to the police?

Three years ago I thought this was a simple question, a matter of he did/she did/they did, a brief detective story. I actually thought I would be able to 'find out the answer'.

In the face of the two women's silence, though, which something in me still grudgingly respects, my question kept opening out into a fan of more complex bewilderments, about women's potential power and why we find seizing it and wielding it so difficult – questions for which I have no answers.

But I know that between 'being made to feel uncomfortable' and 'violence against women' lies a vast range of male and female behaviours. If we deny this, we enfeeble language and drain it of meaning. We insult the suffering of women who have met real violence, and we distort the subtleties of human interaction into caricatures that can serve only as propaganda for war. And it infuriates me that any woman who insists on drawing these crucial distinctions should be called a traitor to her sex.

As for Colin Shepherd's story – even with half the pieces hidden or withheld, it falls into a tragic configuration. The fact is that a certain nexus of forces existed in that place, at that time. The formula was chemical: a precise mix of prissiness, cowardice and brutality. A flick of a fingertip, and up it went. The pieces fell all over the countryside; perhaps they are still falling.

At many points, as I tried to track Colin Shepherd's slow demise, I longed to stop the tape and dream the story to a different, a less cruel and more *useful* ending. If only the Master had gone quietly back to the Lodge with his wife, instead of stepping into the Junior Common Room *to see what the kids were doing*. If only there had been no slow songs. If only Nicole Stewart and Elizabeth Rosen and their friends had developed a bold verbal style to match their sense of dress. If only the judge had had daughters, or a warmer tone of voice. If only the women's supporters had been away on sabbatical leave. If the Vice-Master had run straight into the next-door office with his gown and papers flying. If the Master had been *dashing*, a biter of bullets. If the famous complaints hadn't lain there stinking all summer long, gathering 'agendas' like blowflies.

If only the whole gang of them hadn't been so afraid of life.

Afterword
The Fate of *The First Stone*

Many years ago I came across a remark made by the poet A. D. Hope. He said, 'With hostile critics of my work, I am always scrupulously and cheerfully polite.' Professor Hope's subtle resolution came back to me in March 1995, when my book *The First Stone* finally appeared, and I had to stand up and defend ad nauseam my attempt to discover the truth behind a sexual assault case at one of Melbourne University's residential colleges. I hung on like mad to the poet's tactic, and I'm happy to report that it's possible, in the face of the most intense provocation, to keep your temper for months on end. I bit my lip and gnawed my fist and went on taking deep breaths and counting to ten – partly because I wonder if, when the chips are down, courtesy is all we have left; but also because I knew that, if I waited, a time would come when I could put forward calmly some thoughts about the furore provoked by this book, and about the things I've learnt from the strange experience of publishing *The First Stone*.

Our culture at large is obsessed, at the moment, with matters of sex and power in the relations between women and men. Given this, and given the failed attempt by the two Ormond complainants to get a court to grant them access to the book before its publication, I shouldn't have been surprised by the extent of the response to the book. But what did astonish me, and still does, is the nature of the response – its primal quality. Primal things lie much deeper in people than reason does. People in the grip of a primal response to the very existence of a book like this will read it – and if they consent to read it at all – between the narrow blinkers of anger and fear. I realize now, having had it forced on me by this experience, that there are as many versions of *The First Stone* as there are readers of it. And yet there are certain words and sentences on its pages, put there on purpose in a certain order by the hand of a certain person – namely, me. So I'd like to take the liberty, here, of briefly and firmly listing a few of the things I did not say.

I did not say that the two young women who brought allegations of assault against the Master of their college ought to have agreed to be interviewed by me. I was terribly frustrated that they wouldn't, and in the book I often express this frustration, but right up to the end of the book I continue explicitly to respect their right not to speak to me.

I did not say that women should go back to wearing ankle-length sacks.

I did not say that the correct way to deal with sexual assault or harassment is to knee a man in the balls.

I did not say that women are responsible for the way men behave towards them.

And I most emphatically did not say that women who get raped are asking for it.

I know it's the fate of all writers to feel themselves misread. I hoped I was writing in such a way as to invite people to lay down their guns for a moment and think again – and not only think, but feel again. I wanted people to read in an alert way – alert to things between the lines, things that the law prevents me from saying outright.

The book is subtitled not 'an argument about sex and power', but 'some questions about sex and power'. There are more questions in it than there are answers. Because it declines – or is unable to present itself as one big clonking armour-clad monolithic certainty, it's not the kind of book that's easy to review briskly. Because it's a series of shifting speculations, with an open structure, it's hard to pull out single quotes without distorting it. What the book invites from a reader is openness – an answering spark.

But I found that many people, specially those who locate their sense of worth in holding to an already worked-out political position, are not prepared to take the risk of reading like that. Perhaps they can't, any more. What is not made explicit, for readers like these, is simply not there. Being permanently primed for battle, they read like tanks. They roll right over the little conjunctions and juxtapositions that slither in the undergrowth of the text. It's a scorched-earth style of reading. It refuses to notice the side-paths, the little emotional and psychological byroads that you can't get into unless you climb down from your juggernaut, and take off your helmet and your camouflage gear and your combat boots. It's a poor sort of reading that refuses the invitation to stop reading and lay down the page and turn the attention inwards. And it's always easier, or more comfortable, to misread something, to keep it at arm's length, than to respond to it openly.

Thus, several prominent feminists have used the word 'sentimental' to dismiss the scene in the book where the ex-Master's wife speaks, through inconsolable tears, of the devastation these events have brought to her and her family. Less doctrinaire critics have been able to recognize, in this scene, a terrible example of the human cost of political action which narrows its focus to the purely legal, and thus divorces thought from feeling.

Many feminists, even, incredibly, some who teach in universities, have declared it correct line not to buy *The First Stone* or to read it all. This position is apparently quite widespread, judging by countless reports that have reached me of bitter arguments round dinner tables, in women's reading groups, and at bookshop cash registers. This sort of feminist, while refusing to sully her party credentials by reading the book, also knows, however, or has absorbed from the ether by some osmotic process, exactly what the book 'says', so she is able to pontificate freely on how I have 'betrayed the feminist cause', and 'set feminism back twenty years'. One woman, representing the student body of an institution in the town where I was born, wrote to let me know that, the minute she had heard I was going to write the book, she purged her shelves of all my other books. She rebuked me for having 'profiteered' off other people's misfortunes, and suggested in a challenging tone that I should donate my ill-gotten gains to a worthwhile feminist organization. Here I permitted myself the luxury of a coarse laugh.

The question of money in this context is fascinating. The accusation of 'profiteering' is the last refuge of one's enemy — a reproach densely packed with psychic content. If *The First Stone* had been a jargon-clogged pamphlet bristling with footnotes, if it had sold a comfortably obscure, say, three thousand copies over a couple of years, the response to it from feminism's grimmer tribes would have been much less poisonous. But among those who maintain a victim posture vis à vis the big world, where one can earn an honourable living by writing in a language that the person in the street can understand, nothing is more suspicious than a book which appears to have succeeded.

Crudely, there are two possible attitudes that a hostile feminist might take towards the annoying fact that a lot of people, including feminists of broader sympathy, have defied the girlcott and responded favourably to *The First Stone*. The first one is easy: Garner is a sell-out, a traitor to her sex. She's caved in to the patriarchy and joined the other side. This leaves the grim tribes feeling and looking – to each other, at least – squeaky clean. The other alternative is to wonder whether something might have happened to feminism.

Maybe something's gone wrong.

Maybe something good and important has been hijacked.

Maybe the public debate about women and men has been commandeered by a bulling orthodoxy.

My intention has never been to bash feminism. How could I do that, after what it's meant to me? After what its force and truth make possible? But I hate this disingenuousness, this determination to cling to victimhood at any cost.

Why do the members of this orthodoxy insist that young women are victims? Why do they insist on focusing the debate on only one sort of power – the institutional?

Why do they refuse to acknowledge what experience teaches every girl and woman: that men's unacceptable behaviour towards us extends over a very broad spectrum – that to telescope this and label it all 'violence against women' is to distort both language and experience?

The hysteria that this book has provoked in some quarters reveals clearly and sadly that feminism, once so fresh and full of sparkle, is no different in its habits from any other political theory. Like all belief systems and religions and art forms – like any idea that has the misfortune to have an -ism tacked on to it – feminism has a tendency to calcify, to narrow and harden into fundamentalism. The life spark slips out of it and whisks away, leaving behind it an empty concrete bunker.

To disagree with a fundamentalist feminist, it seems, to question acts carried out in the name of women's rights, is not to challenge her, but to 'betray' her, to turn her into more of a victim than she was already.

One feminist critic in Melbourne put forward the proposition that in telling the Ormond story against the will of the young women involved, I had committed a treachery in the same league as the betrayal of the tribal secrets of the Hindmarsh Island Aboriginal women. The Ormond women, she wrote in the *Australian Book Review,* 'did not want their story told by Helen Garner, writer of fiction making a guest appearance as a journalist. She told their story anyway, has stolen the story that they did not want her to have.'

I find this a piece of the most breathtaking intellectual dishonesty.

In what sense is it 'their' story? It is distorting and deeply wrong to bestow on the Ormond complainants the ownership of this story. It could be truthfully called their story only if they had decided to keep it to themselves, to hold it to themselves as a private trauma. I don't suggest for a single second that they should have done this. And they didn't. They took their complaints to the police. And the police took them to the courts.

Now the law covering sexual assault may still be seriously skewed against women's interests: it plainly is, and I strongly support the correction of this; but a court in a democratic country like Australia is an open forum. Painful as this might be, a court is open. It is open to the scrutiny of the citizens in whose names justice is being aimed at. So, once the complaints reached the courts, the story ceased of necessity to belong to the young women, or to the college, or to the man against whom the allegations were made. It stopped being 'their' story, and it became 'our' story – a new chapter in the endless saga of how we, as a community, try to regulate the power struggle between women and men.

I want now to speak briefly about something called eros.

I used the word rather loosely, perhaps, in the book. You could define eros – if it would stay still long enough for you to get a grip on it – as something lofty and mythological, like 'the gods' messenger', or 'the life spirit'. You could call it the need of things to keep changing and moving on. The Jungians call it 'the spark that ignites and connects'. Eros, most famously, comes bounding into the room when two people fall in love at first sight. But it's also in the excitement that flashes through you when a teacher explains an intellectual proposition and you grasp it – or when someone tells a joke and you get it.

Eros is the quick spirit that moves between people – quick as in the distinction between 'the quick and the dead'. It's the moving force that won't be subdued by habit or law. Its function is to keep cracking open what is becoming rigid and closed-off. Eros explodes the forbidden. Great stand-up comics thrill us by trying to ride its surge. It's at the heart of every heresy – and remember that feminism itself is a heresy against a monolith. Eros mocks our fantasy that we can nail life down and control it. It's as far beyond our attempts to regulate it as sunshine is – or a cyclone.

But one feminist, criticising *The First Stone* in the *Australian,* wants us to accept that 'the dynamics of eros', as she puts it, 'are historically produced'. 'We need,' she says, 'to reconstruct eros between men and women on an equal basis.'

There will always be these moments, I know, when people who think politically and types like me with a metaphysical bent end up staring at each other in helpless silence, with our mouths hanging open.

It's hubristic to speak of 'reconstructing eros'. The whole point of eros, its very usefulness as a concept, is that it's not reconstructable. Eros doesn't give a damn about morals or equality. Though eros moves through the intellect, eros is not intellectual. It moves through politics, but it's not political. It moves between men and women, but it's not in itself sexual. When I talk in the book about eros, I'm trying to talk about that very thing – the thing that's beyond us – the dancing force that we can't control or legislate or make fair.

It's an article of faith among some young feminists that a woman 'has the right' to go about the world dressed in any way she pleases. They think that for a man to respond to – and note, please, that I don't mean to threaten or touch or attack – for a man to respond to what he sees as a statement of her sexuality and of her own attitude to it, is some sort of outrage – and an outrage that the law should deal with. I find the talk of rights in this context quite peculiar. What right are you invoking here? You can only talk about rights, in this context, by pretending that it means nothing at all to wear, say, a lownecked dress in a bar at two o'clock in the morning, or a pair of shorts that your bum's hanging out of on a public beach. To invoke rights, here, you have to fly in the face of the evidence of the senses – as if they believed that each person moved round the world enclosed in a transparent bubble of rights.

And who's going to protect these notional rights? Which regime will provide a line of armed police to make sure that no bloke looks at a woman's breasts with the wrong expression on his face? I'm inviting these young idealists to get real – to grow up – better still, to get conscious. Know what you're doing, what its likely effect is, and decide whether that's what you want. Sexy clothes are part of the wonderful game of life. But to dress to display your body, and then to project all the sexuality of the situation onto men and blame them for it, just so you can continue to feel innocent and put-upon, is dishonest and irresponsible. Worse, it's a relinquishing of power. If a woman dresses to captivate, she'd better learn to keep her wits about her, for when the wrong fish swims into her net.

A woman of my age knows – and it's her responsibility to point this out to younger women – that the world is full of different sorts of men. Many are decent. Some are decent until they start drinking. Many have grown up enough to have learnt manners. Some have taken seriously their responsibility to get conscious. Many men like women, and want to be around them. Some men hate women, and want to be around them. Many have been taught by imagination, or by reason, or by painful or happy experience, that a woman is a person and not just a clump of sexual characteristics put there for them to plunder.

Some men have learnt to recognise and respect the boundary between their fantasy and what is real. Others, trapped in instinct, have not, and never will – and it's a sad fact that we can't depend on the law to make them. Nor will laws alone save us from their depredations, whether trivial or serious. Society makes laws. I am strongly in favour of tough legislation that will give women redress against assault – but around and above and below the laws, for good or ill, there is this fluid element, life. What I'm proposing is that there's a large area for manoeuvre, for the practical exercise of women's individual power, before it's necessary or appropriate to call in the law. And I believe that one of the tasks of feminists should be to expand and develop this area of power.

In the book I describe a photograph. It's a black-and-white shot of a young woman dressed in an elegant and re-vealing gown. I wrote, 'it is impossible not to be moved by her daring beauty. She is a woman in the full glory of her youth, as joyful as a goddess, elated by her own careless au-thority and power.' In response to this page of the book there emerged a grotesque distortion of my intent. One feminist critic, for whom perhaps all gods are vengeful, wrote that my admiring description of this lovely, rather wild young woman was in actual fact an invocation, in modern dress, of that monstrous, punitive, manhating fig-ure of myth – 'vagina dentata in her full glory'.

Other feminists have told me severely that by 'sexualis-ing' young women, I had 'disempowered' them. Leaving aside the hideousness of the language, you don't have to be Camille Paglia to see that this is sick, and mad.

There's been a lot of talk, triggered by the book, about symbolic mothers and daughters. Some feminists have a doom-laden approach to giving maternal advice. The young woman in the beautiful dress is not, they insist, in possession of any power whatsoever, potential or actual, and it is wicked of me to suggest that she might be. For them, only one sort of power is admissible to a discussion of events like these, and that is institutional power. This splendid young woman, then, so clever and lovely and full of life, is nothing but a sad victim. These traumatic events, they solemnly assure her, 'will blight her life'.

What sort of a mother, literal or symbolic, would insist to her daughter that an early experience in the rough adult world, no matter how painful or public, would blight the rest of her life? That is not good mothering. That is pathetic mothering. That is the kind of mothering that doubles the damage. A decent mother, when the dust has settled, would say to her daughter, 'Right. It's over. Now we can look at what's happened. Let's try to analyse what's happened. See how much of what happened was other people's responsibility, and then try to see how much of it, if any, was yours. Take responsibility for your contribution, be it small or large. You are not responsible for men's behaviour towards you, but you are responsible for your own. Pick yourself up now. Wipe your tears. Spit out the bitterness and the blame before they poison you. You're young and clever and strong. Shake the dust of this off your feet. Learn from it, and then move on.'

If all I had to go on, as responses to *The First Stone,* were the critiques of these prominent feminists, I'd be feeling pretty sick by now. But I've had letters, hundreds and hundreds of long, frank letters from strangers. The Melbourne critic (male) who chastised me for writing the book 'to please men' may be interested to know that I estimate the male/female ratio of the letters at about 35/65. I was surprised at how few of them were from cranks or nutcases. By no means did all of these letters – and they're still coming – express blanket approval of the book. But almost all of them were from people who had been prepared to respond to the book in the way I'd hoped – with the defences down – with an answering spark. They're prepared to lay out and re-examine examples, from their own lives, of encounters big and small with the opposite sex, which at the time had bewildered them, or hurt them, or made them angry. I lost count of the people who said, 'I'd like to tell you something that happened to me – or something that I did – many years ago; something that until I read the book I had forgotten – that I'd buried.'

Some of the letters were hilarious. I relate in the book an incident about a masseur at a particular Fitzroy gym who kissed me when I was naked on the table. One woman wrote to me, 'I shrieked when I read about that masseur.' She said the same bloke had kissed her, and that furthermore she'd paid him too, so I wasn't to feel I was the only mug. A man wrote and suggested to me very disapprovingly that I must have led the masseur on. 'Why did you take your clothes off in the massage room,' he sternly asked, 'instead of in the change rooms? What you did was tantamount to striptease.' A masseur who could see as striptease a middle-aged woman scrambling hastily out of a sweaty old tracksuit in a corner gets my prize for sexualising against overwhelming odds.

Some letters, from both men and women, are full of pain, and anger, and shame. Others tell stories of the patient unravelling of interpersonal and institutional knots, and of happy resolutions.

But the word that crops up most frequently is relief: Again and again people speak of the relief they feel that it might be possible to acknowledge that the world of daily work and social life isn't as horrible and destructive and ghastly as punitive feminists insist. People are relieved that it might be possible to admit sympathy in human terms with people on the opposite side of a power divide. They're relieved that ambiguity might be re-admitted to the analysis of thought and action. And specially they're relieved that to admit gradations of offense is not to let the side down or to let chaos come flooding in.

A lot of people have asked me if I regret having written this book – and more particularly, if I regret the letter of ignorant sympathy that I wrote to the Master when I first became aware of the case – the letter that got me into so much trouble, and caused so many doors to be slammed in my face. The answer is no, and no.

One thing I do regret, however, is that my publisher's defamation lawyers obliged me to blur the identity of a certain woman who was the young complainants' chief supporter in the college. I did this in quite a simple way: I didn't invent anything, but each time that the words or actions of this woman appeared in the text, I called her by a different name, thus splitting her into half a dozen people. Months after the book came out, the woman identified herself publicly, to my relief, since I had divided her with the greatest reluctance. This is the only ruse I engaged in, but it has given some people the idea that the book is 'fictionalised' – that it's a novel. It is not a novel. Except for this one tactic to avoid defamation action, it is reportage.

I accept that *The First Stone* has caused pain. I know it's no comfort – that it's almost a cheek – for me to say how sad I am about this. But sometimes a set of events erupts that seems to encapsulate, in complex and important ways, the spirit of its time. These are the stories that need to be told, not swept away like so much debris, or hidden from sight. My attempt to understand this story was frustrated. My version of it is full of holes. But I hope that these holes might, after all, have a use; that through them might pass air and light; that they might even provide a path for the passage of eros; and that they might leave, for women and men who want to think generously about these things, room to move.

About the Author

Helen Garner was born in 1942 in Geelong, Victoria, Australia. After taking a degree in English and French at the University of Melbourne in 1965, she taught in Victorian state high schools for some years, married, and had one child, a daughter.

Since her teaching career ended in 1972, she has worked as a freelance feature journalist, and has published five books of fiction and two of non-fiction. Two of her screenplays have been produced: *Two Friends* (directed by Jane Campion) and *The Last Days of Chez Nous* (Gillian Armstrong).

The First Stone, her non-fiction account of a sexual harassment case at one of Melbourne University's co-ed residential colleges, became an Australian best-seller in 1995, and stirred fierce debate about contemporary relations between men and women.

She has received several Australian literary awards and lives in Sydney.

Other Books by Helen Garner

Monkey Grip (novel) 1977
Honour and *Other People's Children* (two novellas) 1980
The Children's Bach (novel) 1984
Postcards from Surfers (short stories) 1985
Cosmo Cosmolino (novel) 1992
The First Stone (non-fiction) 1995
True Stories (collected essays and journalism) 1996